inside
tumbling

robert ito and
bill roetzheim

HENRY REGNERY COMPANY·CHICAGO

796.47
Roe

Library of Congress Cataloging in Publication Data

Roetzheim, William.
   Inside tumbling.

   Includes index.
   1. Tumbling.   I. Ito, Bob, joint author.   II. Title
GV545.R63   1977   796.4'7   76-42441
ISBN 0-8092-8043-4
ISBN 0-8092-8042-6 pbk.

Photography by Jay Needleman and Sue Lindstrom.
Cover photograph by James Ensigne.

Copyright © 1977 by William Roetzheim and Bob Ito

All rights reserved

Published by Henry Regnery Company

180 North Michigan Avenue, Chicago, Illinois 60601

Manufactured in the United States of America

Library of Congress Catalog Card Number: 76-42441

International Standard Book Number: 0-8092-8043-4 (cloth)

                         0-8092-8042-6 (paper)

Published simultaneously in Canada by

Beaverbooks

953 Dillingham Road

Pickering, Ontario, L1W 1Z7

Canada

acknowledgments

The authors would like to thank Clarence Johnson and Jeff Ko-walcyk, the coach and gymnast from the University of Illinois Chi-cago Circle Campus, for appearing as models. Also appearing are Peggy Mosher, Penny Prellberg, Marla Pearlstein, and Debbie Bleser of the Wilmette Park District Gymnastics team, and their coach, Bob Budnick. Bob Budnick further helped the authors by writing much of the text for Chapter 6 on aerials.

The authors would like to extend their appreciation to Nissen Corporation for permission to reprint the F. I. T. tumbling rules. Thanks also to Mr. Ted Muczyzko, an internationally rated judge, for permission to reprint his system for judging tumbling.

With love to Susan and Devin Ito
and B. J. Roetzheim

contents

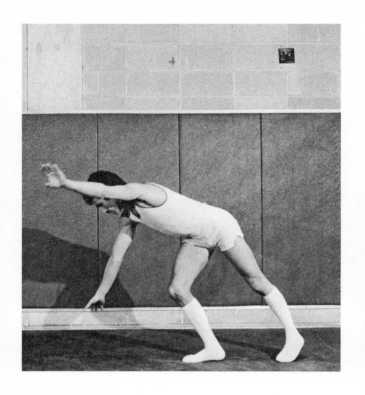

TUMBLING IS AN activity that people have used
throughout history to develop strength,
coordination, and agility.

chapter 1
INTRODUCTION

The origin of tumbling is difficult to trace because few historians have done work in this field. It is a natural tendency to investigate broader areas, such as the overall sport of gymnastics, and not treat tumbling as a separate entity.

It is known that the ancient Greeks used tumbling as a training device to improve their proficiency in combat. Tumbling has also played an important role in the culture of many groups scattered throughout the world. In some African tribes it is an intricate part of tribal ritual. In other areas of the world it was used in relationship to theatrical entertainment and the dance.

Fredrick Ludwig Jahn is given credit for originating the competitive sport of gymnastics. It can be shown that tumbling was a part of his comprehensive physical plan. In the early 1800s Jahn was strongly motivated to help free Germany from French domination under Napoleon. He felt this could only be accomplished by developing the young Germans to be physically, as well as mentally, fit.

The beginning of this activity was crude, with boys performing stunts on apparatus made from tree limbs. As they challenged one another to perform more difficult skills, Jahn carefully recorded how each of these skills was executed. As interest spread, apparatus was manufactured commercially. Groups of athletes sought competition with each other, and a new competitive sport was conceived.

In the 1820s many Germans emigrated to the United States. They brought with them the concept of the sport of gymnastics. They banded together in the large cities and formed athletic clubs that were called Turnvereines. The "Turners" played a major role in introducing physical education into the public schools. Other groups supporting gymnastics in the middle 1800s were the Sokols (Bohemian equivalent of the Turners) and the YMCAs.

The first United States National Tumbling Championship was held in 1886. This was 11 years before a gymnastic All-Around competition was staged. National tumbling competitions were held sporadically from that starting date over the next 22 years. From 1907 until the present time continuous national championships have been held.

Tumbling occupied various positions within the sport of gymnastics. In the '30s in many competitions it was considered part of the all-around. In other meets it was a separate event but counted in the team scoring. During this period it functioned well in contests that also had floor exercise. The skills used in these two events were completely different. Free exercise was performed on the hardwood floor that kept advanced tumbling skills to a minimum. Later when the 40 by 40-foot floor area was padded, tumbling began to occupy a prominent place in routine construction and the two events became repetitious. From that point on, more and more gymnastic meets dropped tumbling from their competitive formats. This void of leadership was corrected in 1973 when the United States Trampoline Association changed its name and incorporated this activity. I should point out that at this time the international sanctioning body for this sport is the Amateur Athletic Union.

Over the years the competitive requirements in tumbling have also changed. In the 1930s and early '40s "cross tumbling routines" were required. These consisted of finishing a tumbling pass in a handstand and from this inverted position, snapping the legs downward to generate momentum for the next routine. The number of trips down the mat has also vacillated. Two routines each composed of four passes were required until the mid-1940s. Later the rules allowed as many trips down the mat as an athlete could take in two minutes. This two-minute requirement was later reduced to a minute and a half. In general a routine now consists of four passes. However, in our federation sponsored meet, the number may vary from two to five, with some being designated as compulsories.

In the last few years the difficulty level in tumbling has advanced rapidly. The greatest difficulty is now being performed by the Soviet acrobats. They have perfected their techniques to a point where they are executing skills thought to be impossible only ten years ago. Recently I watched in amazement as they performed double twists, double backs, laid-out position double backs, and even triple back somersaults.

It is easy to view these advanced Russian tumblers and begin to believe that past United States tumblers performed at a low skill level. This, of course, is not true. Rowland Wolf, as early as the 1930s, was performing the double back. Jack Akins, in the early '40s, was executing a twisting double. Did you know that Jo Ann Matthews, a petite young lady, was turning over twice—as early as 1947? My personal pick as the greatest tumbler of all times would be Irv Bedard. His two-and-one-half twisting back step out to the difficult triple twisting back is hard to duplicate, as are his whip backs into a double twister.

The future of tumbling is easy to predict. National meets now attract greater entries than at any time in the past. Tumbling has come into its own, not just as another gymnastic event, but as a sport that can stand alone.

The tumbling mat used for competition is sixty feet long and five or six feet wide. The mat itself is usually between one and two inches thick and can be composed of any material that will provide a cushioning and resilient surface. Most equipment companies manufacture tumbling mats in one piece that either roll or fold up for storage. Smaller mats (10- to 12-foot lengths) can be linked end to end to form a 60-foot tumbling mat. A regulation floor exercise mat can also be used for practice, but it would not meet official specifications for use in a tumbling meet.

The inner padding of tumbling mats can be composed of many different types of material. Originally hair-felt padding was used in most tumbling mats. During the early and middle '60s a rubber compound similar to that used in wrestling mats was popular. In the late '60s and continuing till now, different types of rigid foam chemical padding have been introduced. These newer pads provide a firm surface for takeoffs and also prevent the tumbler from compressing the pad to the point that he hits the floor.

A properly constructed tumbling mat is a very important consideration for the coach and the athlete. Improperly constructed mats can lead to injuries like twisted ankles, wrist and shin splints, bone bruises, and compression fractures.

The Soviet Union has developed a revolutionary suspension system for tumbling. It is fashioned after the original Reuther concept that uses elastic rebounding surface. When you first observe the mat it appears to be a standard 60-foot tumbling mat, but as soon as you step on its surface, many differences are evident. The entire mat has a springing rebound quality similar to that of a takeoff board. This is accomplished by wood leaf springs set at appropriate intervals below the mat's surface. This springing action enables the tumbler to gain great height while performing difficult stunts. It also allows the tumbler to work an increased number of hours without the manifestation of fatigue or "shin splints." It is only a matter of time until this device is adopted on a universal basis.

The tumbler should choose personal equipment with care and an eye toward comfort and freedom of movement. For young men the first mandatory piece of equipment is a good athletic supporter. A T-shirt, shorts, and cotton socks round out

the usual practice outfit. For competition a sleeveless nylon or knit body shirt with team colors and insignia is mandatory. Either shorts or long competition pants may be worn in meets. In some conferences, socks are mandatory with gymnastics slippers an optional item.

For young women tumbling attire begins with a leotard; tumbling shoes or slippers should be worn. A brassiere should be worn for personal safety when necessary.

As you can see in the illustration, a properly attired tumbler presents a neat appearance that usually will have a positive effect on the judges and spectators. Long hair should be kept out of the face for safety as well as appearance. Remember, tumbling, like gymnastics and diving, is scored by judges who cannot help but be affected by the performer's overall appearance. A neat appearance with a clean attractive uniform will help put the judges in a better frame of mind while scoring your routine. In some states at the high school level judges have the option of deducting points *before* the routine starts for an improperly uniformed athlete.

EVERY TUMBLER should be spotted when learning new tricks.

chapter 2
SPOTTING AND SAFETY TECHNIQUES

Spotting is the assisting of performers while they are executing stunts in order to prevent injuries and speed learning.

Every tumbler should understand as much as possible about spotting. If the tumblers are familiar with all spotting techniques, they can better choose the method that will help them learn. They can also help one another when their coach is working with a different tumbler.

There are two basic types of spotting techniques: hand spotting, where the coach actually manipulates the student through the movement; and belt spotting, where the student is strapped into a belt attached to ropes.

Belt spotting is by far the safest technique. When applying this method the coach or spotter has complete control over the tumbler's body throughout the trick. The spotter can stop the trick anytime there is danger by pulling on the ropes. At no point during difficult stunts is the tumbler

out of the spotter's immediate close control. There are three general classifications of belts: hand belts, overhead spotting belts, and twisting belts.

Hand belts are useful in spotting tricks where the coach must stay close to the tumbler (*e.g.,* standing back flips). Also, if individual spotters are not strong enough to handle the student alone, the hand belt allows two people to spot the same tumbler simultaneously. The disadvantage of hand belts is the restriction placed on the student's movements. The spotters must stand very close to the student and may get in the way during the trick. The spotter also has no mechanical advantage and must depend on sheer strength to keep the performer from falling.

Overhead spotting rigs are far superior. You can protect the tumbler when he is doing very high tricks that are beyond the reach of a hand operated belt. When using an overhead rig, the coach can also spot a

long series of difficult tricks without hampering the tumbler's movement. The biggest disadvantage of the overhead spotting rig is the extra weight of the belt and long ropes. Also, the ropes can become entangled in the tumbler's arms during twisting moves or double somersaults.

Tumblers use twisting belts whenever learning a trick that requires twisting and flipping at the same time. Without the development of the twisting belt it would be very dangerous to learn many difficult tumbling stunts like the "double" or "triple

A TWISTING BELT prevents entanglement in the ropes.

twist." Twisting belts weigh more than regular belts, and this excess weight can become a real problem when training young athletes. Ball bearings are used to make the twisting mechanism work. You must handle these belts carefully, for if the ball bearings become dented the entire twisting mechanism will stick.

Hand spotting techniques, when used properly by an experienced coach, can greatly speed learning for young tumblers. There are no belts or ropes to put on or take off. The tumbler doesn't lose practice time changing into and out of equipment. The coach can also spot more than one student without waiting for them to change into the belt.

From the tumbler's point of view hand spotting has distinct advantages over belt spotting. All belt spotting equipment has a certain amount of weight that the tumbler must adjust to. In addition, the student must also adjust to the ropes. When a proficient coach hand spots a trick, the student doesn't have these adjustments to make.

An experienced coach will usually prefer hand spotting techniques because he can quickly correct mistakes by forcing the tumbler into correct positions *during* each trick. For example, if during a back somersault the tumbler keeps throwing his head back too soon, a spotter using belts could only make the tumbler aware of the mistake after it occurred. A good hand spotter could correct the mistake during the trick by holding the tumbler's head to prevent it from going back.

Once the student begins to understand a trick and perform each part correctly, the coach can gradually withdraw the hand spot so as to ease the student into performing the stunt by himself. This type of technique would be especially useful when trying to master very difficult or dangerous stunts.

On any particularly difficult stunt the student might balk at an attempt without

any spotting. This could set up an extra mental barrier to his ever mastering the stunt. A good coach can avoid this barrier by gradually withdrawing the spot as the tumbler's confidence increases.

Often we have observed that the only barrier between a good tumbler and a difficult trick is a lack of confidence. The athlete is "psyched out." The coach's duty during spotting is more than just the physical job of helping a gymnast. It is his decision to determine whether the athlete is ready emotionally, as well as physically, to perform the new stunt. It is important to understand that spotting and emotional/mental evaluations by the coach go hand in hand. The

tumbler's physical capabilities sometimes outstrip his emotional or mental readiness to perform a new skill. Learning a new tumbling skill is like walking for the first time. A poorly prepared tumbler may suddenly realize his body is performing a new, risky maneuver; and he may panic. An observant coach understands this and with judicious use of spotting techniques helps the athlete overcome his fears. He also convinces the tumbler that he can perform the trick alone, so when the student asks, "Can I do it, Coach?" they both know he can.

Spotting is a physical skill that, like any other sport skill, must be learned and practiced in order to be perfected. Obviously

ACTIVE SPOTTING CAN be used for advanced tumbling moves.

one cannot start with the more difficult or dangerous tricks (*e.g.,* double backs, double fulls, etc.). This would be like learning to drive a car at the Indianapolis 500—a disaster!

Most competent spotters learned their techniques at the same time and at the same rate that they learned tumbling skills. Students learn to spot each new trick so as to progress faster. As the tricks become more advanced so do the spotting skills. After a year or so, good tumblers with sufficient body size can do a fair job of spotting flip-flops or back flips, or even full twists with the overhead rig. It is not absolutely necessary to be a tumbler in order to spot tumbling, although it helps. Anyone who is willing to put in a lot of time and effort can learn to spot. As tricks become more difficult, the spotting must be more sophisticated.

Aiding a performer can be further subdivided into "passive" and "active" spotting.

Coaches using a passive spotting technique wait for the tumbler to make a mistake and react with an assist or catch. When spotting in an active manner, the coach begins assistance on the takeoff and continues the spot all the way through the landing.

The advantage of active spotting is that it helps the student quickly acquire the correct "feel" of each trick. Active spotting is also safer than passive spotting. The coach has his hands on the gymnast throughout the trick. In passive spotting the coach only reacts to mistakes. Obviously the margin for error is smaller in active spotting because no one's reactions are immediate.

Passive spotting does have a place in the coach's repertoire. After mastering a trick with active spotting methods, the student may need the coach's passive presence near the mat for confidence.

During the early learning process active spotting is definitely the best method available to speed up the learning process. Active spotting requires skill and experience on the part of the coach but is well worth the efforts in terms of results and safety.

The authors have spent countless hours in different gyms—working out, competing, and coaching. Every time we see a new spotting technique we absorb as much of it as possible and store it away for future use. Don't over-commit yourself to one style or type of spotting. Each new student you help may require a slightly different approach. Like all good teachers we are "pack rats" of information. Whenever we observe an effective, safe spotting method it is filed away. Watch experienced coaches and learn from them.

The tumbler places total reliance on his spotters. The student can be in a very dangerous position during difficult, advanced stunts. As a spotter you must follow one ironclad rule, a rule that can never be ignored or taken lightly. "If anyone gets hurt while being spotted, it should be the spotter." A coach who has developed this attitude may get bumped, bruised, or occasionally injured, but that is an acceptable risk. The safety of the students is the coach's paramount responsibility. If each coach spotted every athlete as he would his own children, the incidence of injuries would decrease and tumblers would have the confidence necessary to learn quickly.

The newest developments in gymnastics and tumbling safety equipment are crash pads and landing mats. Crash pads are large pieces of soft foam rubber covered with nylon and usually from 12 to 16 inches thick. Landing mats are medium soft pieces of foam rubber covered with nylon. They vary in thickness from four to six inches.

Crash pads are used either singly or in stacks to protect against falls. If the tumbler makes a mistake and lands on his back or neck on crash pads, the chance of serious injury is very slight. In fact, there are teaching progressions for tricks (*e.g.*,

IN THE FOREGROUND is a four-inch landing mat, in the background a typical eight-inch crash pad. Both are invaluable pieces of safety equipment.

double back) that opt for crash pads as opposed to either belts or hand spots.

Landing mats do not provide as much protection in case of a missed trick. In fact, they were not designed for that purpose. These special mats are used to decrease the landing shock to the legs after a particularly high or fast movement.

In most tumbling competitions, crash pads or landing mats cannot be used without a point deduction. No gym, however, would be complete without several of these very necessary pieces of equipment. Next to a coach, a crash pad can be the tumbler's best friend.

FUNDAMENTALS ARE THE foundation
of proper tumbling.

chapter 3
THE FUNDAMENTALS OF TUMBLING

Every athlete, no matter what his sport, has to master a set of fundamental skills. In an event like track and field, the basic skills that are perfected are running, jumping, and throwing. In tumbling, the beginner must learn from scratch all but a few of the fundamental skills. The difference between these two sets of fundamentals is too important to pass over without further comment. Every athlete, in fact every normal healthy person, can run, jump, and throw. The basic skills for tumbling, however, must be taught from the beginning. Because advanced tumbling stunts are based entirely on the fundamentals, learning the basics properly is doubly important for the novice tumbler.

The basic skills can be placed in one of three general groups or categories. They are: flexibility movements, position movements, and fundamental tricks.

The flexibility movements develop the spinal, hip, thigh, and shoulder flexibility necessary to tumble properly and safely. A complete flexibility routine when used as a warm-up will prepare the tumbler for more vigorous activity. A flexible athlete will also be able to avoid injuries like pulled muscles or sprained ankles.

The position movements stress certain body alignments that are absolutely necessary for advanced tumbling. A tumbler can perform routines with improper body position without ever being aware of the mistake. Simple repetition may not correct the improper position. If the athlete relies on repeated attempts to gradually develop a "feel" for correct body alignment, many weeks will be wasted practicing a bad habit. Learn correct body position first so as to save time and effort.

The fundamental tricks are familiar to most people. Although the first basic tricks are not difficult, they are very important. The forward and backward rolls, for instance, help develop a proper tuck position.

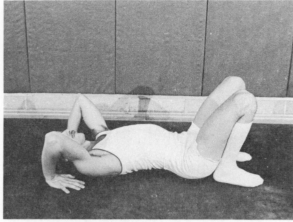

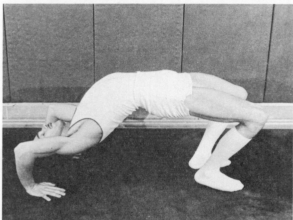

That position is very important when the advanced tumbler attempts a double backward somersault. The last fundamental trick is the backward handspring, which is in 75 to 80 percent of all individual tumbling runs. The novice tumbler should not take shortcuts when learning these fundamental skills.

FLEXIBILITY MOVEMENTS

These movements are included to help you develop the suppleness you will need in tumbling. Remember these movements do not constitute a complete warm-up. In fact a warm-up of 15 minutes should precede any type of workout.

Backbend

The backbend will help you develop the shoulder and back flexibility necessary to learn tricks like flip-flops and headsprings. You should attempt the backbend from a lying down position. Straighten the arms and legs while looking back toward the mat, pushing the body into a high arch.

At first you may not be able to straighten the arms and legs completely. Don't worry. As your flexibility increases you will be able to properly execute this skill.

Once you have mastered the backbend you may try the next step, which is to lower from a standing position directly to the backbend. This should be practiced at first with a spotter. You may also lower onto a built up platform of cushions.

Remember, it is very important to allow the lower body to move forward to counterbalance the backward momentum of this trick. Keep the arms straight and keep your head in a neutral position.

Limbers

The next step in the backbend sequence is the limber, both forward and backward. To perform a back limber stand with both hands overhead and lower down to a backbend trying to get your hands as close to your feet as possible. The split second your hands hit the mat, push off with your feet passing through the handstand and land on your feet.

To perform a front limber start with your hands overhead, one foot in front of the other. Place your hands on the mat and kick to a handstand. As you overbalance,

BACKBEND

WHEN PERFORMING THE front limber, be sure to pass through a momentary handstand.

hyperextend your back, placing your feet on the mat as close to your hands as possible. Allow your hips to move forward and raise up, keeping the arms overhead and your head back.

Walkovers

After you can perform the front and back limbers, the final steps in this series are the walkovers. To begin the back walkover, stand with one foot in front of the other and your arms overhead. As you hyperextend your back and your body begins rotating in a backward direction, move your arms and

upper body back as the lead leg moves upward. The lead leg acts as a counterbalance, allowing you to keep the support leg straight. Just before the hands reach the floor the support leg pushes off the mat.

Remember to keep the arms overhead and straight. Avoid quick movements of the head or you will lose control of your body. This lack of control will cause your hands to contact the ground at a distant point from the feet. Once both feet leave the ground, the legs should pass through a split position while the body is supported on the hands.

Start the front walkover with the arms extended overhead. Step forward on to one leg, placing the hands on the mat close to the feet while kicking the back leg upward (the body passes through a front scale position). The first leg touches the ground as close to the hands as possible. When the second leg moves overhead, shift your hips forward toward the supporting foot and use the second leg as a counterbalance to lift the upper body off the ground.

Remember to keep the arms straight and the head at least neutral. If you bring the head or arms forward too soon you will lose back flexion, which will cause you to collapse.

Front Scale

At first glance the front scale may appear to

be unrelated to tumbling and closer to dance or gymnastics. However, several important tumbling moves require that you pass through the front scale position.

Stand with your hands above your head, step forward and lower the body while raising the back leg. You are in the correct position when your body is arched and your back leg and head are about in alignment.

Both the support leg and the back leg should be straight. Always practice the front scale on both sides or you will never increase the flexibility of your weaker side.

Front Splits

Young women interested in acrobatics and tumbling seldom have trouble learning forward splits on both sides, as well as pancake splits. Women are usually flexible and will learn splits without prompting from their coach. Young men, however, are not as flexible as women and usually balk when this skill is introduced.

Hamstring flexibility is important to all

tumblers. One of the best ways to improve hamstring flexibility is through the practice of splits.

To perform the splits, place one foot in front of your body and the other leg behind. Lower down as far as possible while trying to keep the knees straight. The back part of the forward leg and the front part of the rear leg should be touching the mat.

When you first attempt to learn the splits, be careful not to overstretch the muscles. It is always better to go a little slower at first.

POSITION MOVEMENTS

Handstand

The handstand is a basic for gymnastics and tumbling. In gymnastics the handstand must be held steady for at least two seconds. However, for tumbling we are not interested in holding a balanced handstand. There are no static or hold positions in tumbling, so the handstand is used to acquaint the student with proper handstand position.

A correct handstand is held with the arms at shoulder width, elbows straight and the entire body stretched above the hands. If the legs are bent or the back is arched, the body will be too loose and you will have trouble moving through this position quickly.

Mule Kick

The third position movement is the mule kick. The mule kick or snap-down is a very important skill because it is part of the backward handspring. The backward handspring is used during 75 to 80 percent of all difficult tumbling runs; therefore, learning the mule kick is very important.

The mule kick begins in a stretched handstand position with the body leaning toward the mat. Snap both legs down to the mat aiming for a point close to your supporting hand position. Simultaneously

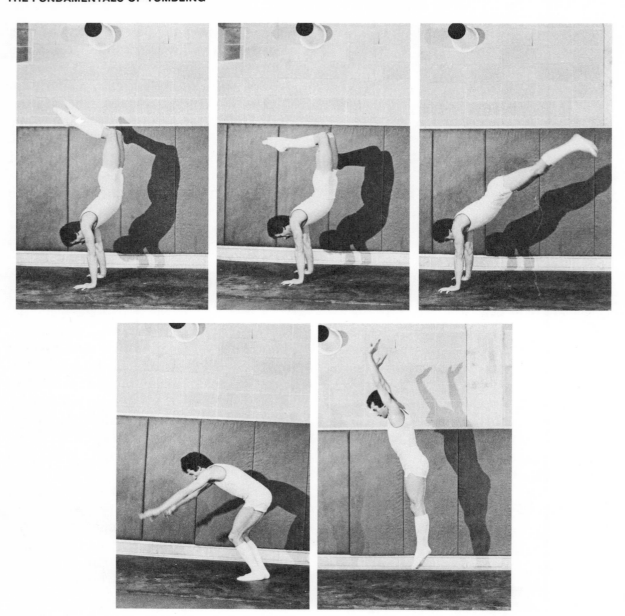

push hard with the arms. Land on your feet with the arms overhead and the body completely vertical.

Throughout the mule kick keep the body tight and under control. If your back is arched or your body loose, the mule kick will be very weak and slow. As you become accustomed to this movement, try to increase your speed and power and add a jump or rebound after your feet hit.

All of the position movements should be practiced over and over again. Even after you have mastered these skills, continued practice will help your devlopment as a

tumbler. They can easily be incorporated into your warm-up on a regular basis.

FUNDAMENTAL TRICKS

Chances are, the first two or three fundamental tricks are things you tried as a youngster. These tricks are listed in the proper order in which they should be learned. Aside from the fact that these tricks increase in difficulty, several moves help you learn skills that are prerequisites for following stunts. It is important not to skip over a trick that you find difficult. To

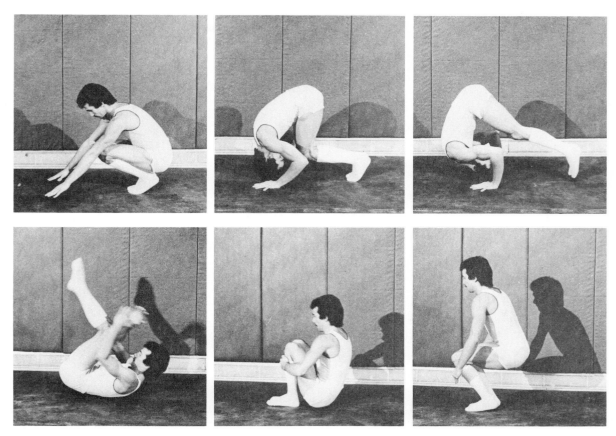

be a good tumbler take a hint from the training of all good professional athletes; become so proficient in fundamental tumbling that you can perform each movement literally blindfolded.

Forward Roll

There are two very important reasons for learning a forward roll: First, you learn to use a tuck position that is an important part of backward somersaults; second, if you ever lose your balance while moving forward, you can avoid injury by quickly doing a forward roll.

The trick should have a smooth, rolling feeling without any part of the body slapping or bumping the mat. From a squat position place your hands on the floor, fingers extended forward. The back of the head should be the first body part making contact with the floor. As your weight is transferred to your rounded back, grab both legs (tuck) compressing the body into a tight ball.

Backward Roll

The backward roll is used less often than the forward roll, but also stresses the tuck position and is a safety trick if you lose your balance while moving backwards. The beginner should start this trick from a sitting position. The chin should be forced down upon the chest and the back should be rounded. As the body moves backward, place the hands on either side of the head, fingers pointed forward. Push downward with the hands in order to obtain ground clearance for the head. There will be a tendency as you push to extend the body. Fight this impulse and remain tucked.

Cartwheel

The cartwheel is the first trick you will attempt from a standing position with a one foot takeoff. To determine if you should begin the cartwheel to the left or right use this simple test. Get into a track starting position; you will find in most cases the

bent leg determines the direction the trick will take. If your left leg is bent perform in that direction; if your right leg is the bent leg work to your right.

Draw a line about five feet long. Place both feet on this line. If you perform a cartwheel to the left, the left hand will be placed on this line close to the performer followed by the right hand which should also contact this line. When first exercising this skill you can allow the legs to pass at a lower angle, but as you gain proficiency they should pass directly over the head.

Later you can vary the side characteristics of this move by starting the cartwheel facing forward and ending the trick facing backwards. While on your hands keep your legs apart and your knees straight.

Round-Off

The round-off is the first "intermediate" trick that you will learn. The round-off enables you to convert forward running momentum into backward motion. It is a trick that tumblers learn early in training but it is seldom perfected until a tumbler is advanced.

You will begin to learn the round-off by landing a cartwheel on two legs facing in the direction from which you started. As you become more comfortable with this landing, bring the legs together in the handstand position before snapping them down to the mat. The hand placement for a round-off is also slightly different than for a cartwheel. In figure 1a you see the hand

WHEN LEARNING A round-off from a stand, it is important to get the legs together while the body is as close to vertical as possible.

placement for a cartwheel. In figure 1b you see the hand position for a round-off.

The difference in the placement of the second hand for the round-off allows you to complete the half twist while the body is still supported on your hands.

The final step in learning the round-off is to add first a few steps and finally a strong run before the trick. When you begin performing this skill from a run you should learn a tumbler's hurdle. This skipping movement enables you to efficiently convert your run into a powerful round-off. The arms are thrust upward in conjunction with the skip. If you performed the cartwheel to the left, the left leg should lead during this skipping movement.

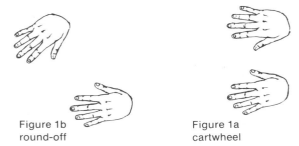

Figure 1b
round-off

Figure 1a
cartwheel

The next three tricks in this progression of fundamentals are variations of the *kip*. The kip is a basic movement in tumbling and gymnastics. When you learn the kip in one form you can easily learn the other forms of this movement. The kip is characterized by a quick change in the body from a pike to an arched position.

Kip-Up

The kip-up is not actually a tumbling stunt but it will help us learn to coordinate the pike to arch movement. Begin the kip-up in a sitting position. Roll backwards pulling the feet overhead in a pike position with your hands on the mat next to your head, fingers extended forward. Allow your hips to roll forward slightly before extending the body from a pike to an arch and pushing with your arms. It is extremely important to begin quickly, extending the legs out of the piked position before pushing with the hands against the floor. Once you have performed the extension and push there is nothing more that can be done to improve

KIP-UP

or add to the power of a trick. It is most important that you hold your body in the stretched position with your arms extended until the landing.

Head Spring (from a piked headstand)

Beginning with this trick we will teach progressions for all the remaining fundamentals. The first part of the headspring progression is the piked headstand. Make sure that your hands and head form a triangle on the mats.

Lean the entire body forward (toward the head) until you are approximately at a 45-degree angle. This shifting of the weight to the back of the head is extremely important. Then extend and push, holding your position.

This is probably the most difficult way to perform a headspring. You will need a spotter to help. However, if you can master this, the standing headspring will be much easier, because of the leg thrust.

After you are able to perform the headkip from a headstand, start the movement from a squat position. Pushing into the piked handstand with the legs will add power and momentum to the trick. Remember to work off the back portion of the head. When you can perform the squat headspring, smoothly start the stunt from a standing position. Despite the different starting points, the actual technique of the headkip is never changed.

Front Handspring

The handspring will be split into two parts: the power phase, and the flight phase, which includes the landing.

In the first part of the progression you will kick to a stretched handstand against resistance. Try to hit the spotter's arm with as much force as possible centered in the legs. Try to have the legs come together within 10 degrees of the handstand position. Don't dive onto your hands but exercise control in their placement.

Now using the power technique described above, kick to a handstand imagining that the spotter's arm is still there. Hold

HEADSPRING

the stretched handstand while the spotter assists in the flight and landing.

Backward Handspring

The backward handspring or flip-flop is the most important single trick that you will learn. In a typical tumbling routine, three out of the four runs are usually backward tumbling sequences. In 99 percent of all backward runs, you will use the flip-flop as part of the sequence. The power, rhythm, and beauty of expert tumbling depend on mastery of the backward handspring. Because the backward handspring is so important, we will explain two different methods for learning this trick. Each method offers different advantages; both, however, should be tried for maximum benefit.

Sit-Lean Progression

Start in a standing position with the arms at your side, knees bent slightly. Simultaneously, lean backwards and swing your arms to the rear. When you begin to lose balance, swing the arms up and overhead; push with your legs and attempt to land in a handstand. Push off your hands and pull the feet under, landing with your arms extended overhead.

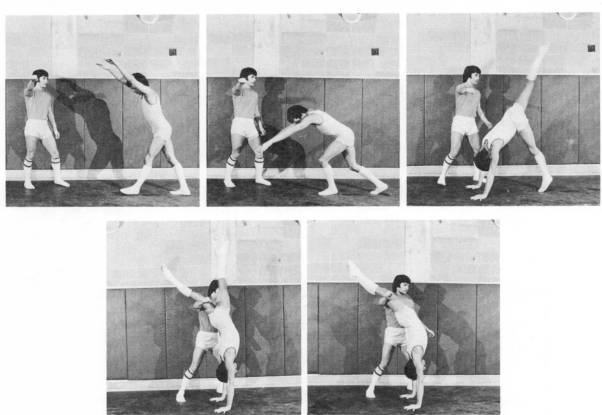

THIS KICK TO a handstand drill will build power for . . .

. . . the front handspring.

PRACTICE THE SIT-LEAN position before the complete movement.

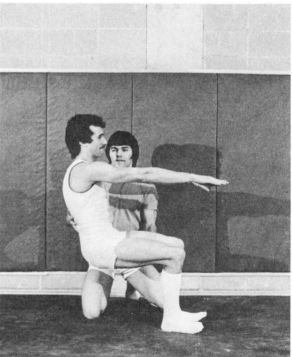

Flip-flops are not fast backbends, nor are they the type of trick that requires a great deal of flexibility. At one point during the trick, the feet and hands should be off the mat. However, you should not try to get a lot of height in this trick. The important thing to remember about flip-flops is that they should cover distance down the mats during the trick. Once you perfect a standing flip-flop, performing a correct flip-flop out of a round-off is easier because you will already have developed backward momentum.

Mule-Kick Progression

The second progression begins in a stretched handstand position. Pull your feet down and push with your arms, landing on your feet and leaning backwards. As soon as your feet land, throw your arms back to the mat; immediately push off your legs, landing in a handstand. Again pull your feet down and push with your arms, landing on your feet with your arms overhead.

In both methods you should always be spotted closely until you are able to safely perform the movements alone. The be-

WHEN PRACTICING A flip-flop, *always* rebound as high as possible afterwards

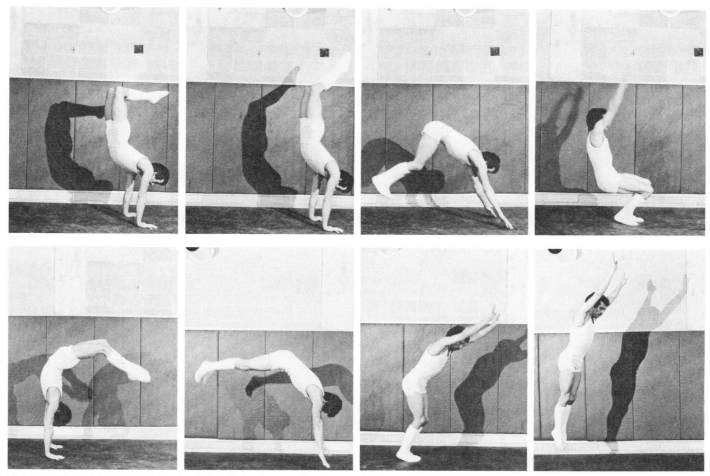

MULE-KICK PROGRESSION. During this drill, try to move backwards down the mat.

ginner should keep his arms straight and avoid throwing the head back too hard. In all backward handsprings try to cover more than the length of your own body. You should stretch and take distance in the first phase of this trick and attempt to shorten the distance between hands and feet.

The advantage of the sit-lean progression is that it seems less formidable to the young or inexperienced tumbler. It also requires less overall strength to perform. Most tumblers learn the flip-flop using this method. The second procedure requires more strength than the first. But, it also re-produces the exact feel of performing a flip-flop in a sequence of tricks.

All of the fundamental movements we have discussed are very important to the beginning tumbler. The intermediate or advanced tumbler can also benefit from continued practice of the fundamentals. After a general warm-up, several standing flip-flops or headsprings from a headstand will sharpen your timing and strengthen your arms and legs. Some of the basic movements may not make sense at first. Continued practice will lay a good foundation for advanced tumbling.

chapter 4
SOMERSAULTS

All tumbling "passes" must have at least three consecutive tricks to be effective in competition. A three-trick pass can be divided into two basic parts. The first part is the lead-up where the athlete tries to build momentum and power; the second segment is usually a high somersault or flip that ends the routine. The lead-up tricks are hand-springs, round-offs, flip-flops, and also low, open, back flips. Except for beginners the final trick in tumbling sequences can be a high single or a double somersault or possibly a twisting flip.

A somersault or flip is a stunt where the tumbler rotates 360 degrees either forward, backward, or sideways, from feet to feet. There are three body positions that one can use while attempting a somersault: the tuck, the layout, and the pike positions.

The most common position used during flips is the tuck. In a tuck position the athlete bends both knees up to the chest and grabs the legs just below the knees. While in

this position the tumbler can decrease the total length of his body, thus achieving a faster spin throughout the flip. Most coaches will teach this position when they introduce flips to new students. Besides the increased spin one can attain in the tuck, the coach has an easier time spotting this compact position.

The layout position is usually used only with single flips. While in a layout position the tumbler demonstrates a pleasant symmetrical look, but his elongated body reduces the speed of rotation far below the level enjoyed while being tucked. The layout position is also a very important prerequisite for twisting somersaults. It is very difficult to twist and flip while in a tucked or piked position; it also doesn't look very pleasing. Therefore, you must learn the lay-out so you can advance into the more difficult twisting somersaults at a later time.

The pike is the last type of flipping position. Although it is very important in gym-

27

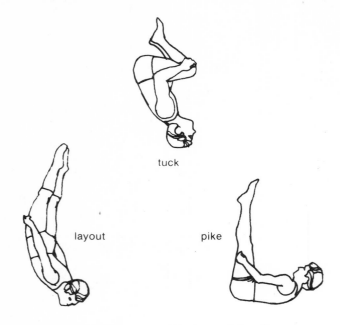

tuck

layout

pike

nastics techniques, the tight pike is not very popular among tumblers. First of all it is a difficult position to work out of, and it is also difficult to twist while in a tight pike. The "open pike" position is more prevalent in floor exercise routines but can be used for tumbling; however, the extra height needed to perform piked somersaults will absorb your power, reducing your efficiency in a long routine. You will normally see piked (open or closed) tricks at the very beginning or end of a tumbling pass.

The first two somersaults you will learn are the back flip and the front flip, both performed in a tuck position. Some coaches prefer to teach the front flip first because it doesn't frighten novice tumblers as much as a back "somy." The authors feel that a back flip should be learned first for several reasons. First, three fourths of every tumbling routine consists of backward movements; second, it takes less strength and power to perform back routines than forward sequences.

BACKWARD SOMERSAULT

Before actually attempting a backward flip the novice tumbler should master the steps in the following lead-up drill. This drill will establish the proper takeoff with enough rotation to complete the trick.

In the first part of the drill the tumbler simply swings his arms up and simultaneously jumps as high as possible. Then he repeats this several times with the coach adding extra lift. This simulates the take-off action for a proper back flip.

In the next step the student jumps up, and, as the feet leave the ground, he brings the knees up to the chest (leaving the arms overhead and the head neutral). This will

BE SURE TO keep your arms above your head throughout the drill.

cause the tumbler to begin rotating backward on the spotter's hands; it is the initiation of the flipping action.

When the tumbler can perform both steps of this drill with control and consistency, the coach should shift his spotting positions as illustrated below.

Now applying this drill, a proficient spotter can judge when the tumbler begins to rotate and allows his head to move backward while pulling his knees up and over. With this aid the student will have little difficulty executing the tucked back. If the instructor is not well trained, he should use a spotting belt.

It is not unusual to see a beginner attempt a back flip by laying his head back without using the arms for lift or grabbing

his tuck. This results in a very low, poorly executed trick. If it becomes a habit, it can permanently hamper the tumbler's progress. On occasions experienced tumblers will make the same mistake of prematurely moving the head back when they feel insecure during a trick. No one wants to land on his head, so they "pull" the head through the somersault quickly. To avoid this problem athletes and coaches should understand that correct somersault techniques require a lifting motion and only after this movement has begun should a tumbler attempt to increase rotation.

The direction, height, and amount of flip for each trick are determined at the instant the tumbler leaves the ground. In other words, if you leave the ground with your arms up and head neutral, your direction will be up. If you leave the ground with your head back and/or your body leaning back, your direction will be back.

Generally, the tumbler's force against the floor, coupled with the position of the arms, head, and upper body, will all play a role in determining the height and general trajectory of the stunt. In a tuck back, the initial flipping action is initiated by pulling the knees upward, causing the body to begin rotating. During this phase the arms and upper body can reach for maximum height while the lower body initiates the flip. When the "crest" of the trick is reached, the somersault movement is completed by moving the head back and grabbing a tuck.

Each different somersault will require the tumbler to learn how to gain height with the arms and initiate flip with body movement other than initiated by the head and shoulders. The body follows the head; therefore, a double somersault performed by a tumbler moving his head back too quickly will result in inadequate lift and could be most dangerous.

In a backward tuck, the knees initiate the flip. In a back pike, the lifting of the thigh begins your rotation while the dominant turning factor is the hyperextended back (arched). As you experiment with these different positions you may find that you must think in terms of a different concept to feel or explain these movements.

Coaching a sport as complicated as tumbling will require ingenuity, flexibility, and creativity. Remember that youngsters usually learn these movements by constant repetition and the "feel" of the move. The actual technique that you read here or can discern from our sequence photos may make little or no sense to an athlete. Be observant and willing to vary approaches, so long as you know your ultimate goal and are always moving in that direction. Trust the athlete to recognize technique by its

"feel" rather than exact scientific explanations.

Throughout this book you will have two yardsticks with which to measure your coaching or performing. The first is the sequence photography and artwork. The second is the explanations written in the text of each chapter. The photographs show the proper technique as it is actually performed by competent tumblers. The text is a condensed version of our coaching views that have successfully helped our students "feel" their way through new moves. At times the pictures may seem to contradict the explanations or vice versa. We are aware of this and are simply giving the tumbler and coach previously tested information to work with.

Working Into and Out of Back Flips

Before we discuss the details of working back flips into a series, there is an important concept all tumblers should understand. We will call this the concept of "positive movement" in tumbling. A properly executed series of tumbling tricks will cover a good distance in a straight line down the tumbling mat. A tumbler, after a powerful round-off flip-flop, will raise his body eight or more feet off the ground. This is much higher than the tumbler can actually jump without tumbling. In fact, it is higher than the world record for high jump. In the 1950s several enterprising tumblers from the University of Illinois at Champaign-Urbana put on half-time demonstrations where all the tumblers would break the high jump record by as much as several inches. (We should mention, in all fairness, that track and field performers are required to use a one-foot takeoff and don't tumble to build power.) The whole point to this little story is the fact that through power tumbling with "positive movement" you can get many times higher than by jumping.

Specifically, a tumbler will try to initiate

movement in a straight line while simultaneously adding the speed of constant 360 degree rotation. At the point of takeoff, all of this straight line and rotary power and speed can be converted to height and spin by changing the angle between the feet and center of gravity.

The correct angle between the feet and center of gravity during round-offs, flip-flops, or whipback flips enables the tumbler to build power in a straight line.

Just before takeoff of the last stunt, this angle will be changed to convert the "straight line" force into height.

This technique can be compared to the action of throwing a ball against the corner of a wall and floor. The sudden change in trajectory when the ball hits the corner forces it high into the air. The rapid change in angle (or blocking) that is employed by the tumbler helps him to gain great height.

This idea of "positive movement" operates in all tumbling sequences, both forward and backward. Usually it takes from several months to two years before tumblers understand this concept and become strong and skilled enough to place it into practice.

The average tumbling student wants to learn back (and front) flips quickly and will sometimes attempt these tricks before mastering some necessary fundamentals.

A good way to learn a lift back flip is to practice with a flip-flop back flip from a stand.

Step 1. From a standing position, the gymnast will perform a flip-flop with an immediate rebound jump. This rebound jump is very fast and performed without much knee bend. Be sure to have the arms overhead throughout the jump for greater height.

Step 2. With the coach standing behind, the student performs a flip-flop rebound, raising the knees toward the chest. This will start the back flip rota-tion while maintaining good lift or height (remember to keep the arms overhead).

Step 3. In the final step, the spotter will assist from the side while the tumbler performs step 1 and 2 with more power and speed. After the student feels he is flipping backwards (step 2) he accelerates and completes the flip by moving the head back and bringing the knees to the hands. Remember to "block" so that the body leaves the ground at the proper angle. If you pull your feet through, throw your head too early, or forget to lift your arms, the back flip will be either low or underspun.

This complete drill should be performed regularly by beginning and advanced students. The value of the drill is that it forces the tumbler to rely on proper technique, rather than strength or a fast lead-up run. A good variation of this drill would be to add flip-flops before the back flip. Start with one backward handspring to a back flip and add flip-flops on each turn until you are performing five or six before the somersault. Then work your way down until reaching one flip-flop to a back "somy." We have found this an excellent way to learn power tumbling quickly and safely; it also increases endurance and overall strength.

Another good training technique is to start with a round-off, flip-flop, back flip, and add a flip-flop until you can do a round-off, five flip-flops and a back flip. Then work your way back down, taking away one flip-flop at a time until you get to one. While performing this drill (and the previous one), try to maintain the same momentum and speed during the entire row of flip-flops.

Tumblers will be learning how to work into a back flip at the same time that they are perfecting the technique for a round-off flip-flop. Try to avoid the temptation to

THE COMPLETED "DRILL" will build tumbling power faster than **any** other method.

learn a round-off, back flip before you have perfected a round-off, flip-flop and a flip-flop back flip from a stand. Novice tumblers find it easier, at first, to perform a back flip after a round-off, because they use the momentum of the lead-up run instead of a properly executed flip-flop. The round-off back sequence is not used very much in tumbling, and it can make it harder to learn round-off flip-flops or back flips, out of backward handsprings. Again we caution you to learn correct fundamentals first, before learning more difficult stunts.

After mastering a correctly executed round-off, flip-flop, back flip, you will begin learning how to put back flips in the middle of a series of tricks. If you use a high back flip in the middle of a series it is very difficult to work out of it. Any high somer-

sault will "use up" the backward movement you need to continue performing tricks.

The middle flips have to be "whip" flips that continue moving down the mats. A whip back is low between shoulder and rib height, and it is always performed in a layout position. The characteristics that differentiate this skill from a true layout are their lack of amplitude and vigorous piking of the legs in toward the body just prior to landing. Instead of blocking before the takeoff you pull your feet through so as to keep moving backward for the next trick. The body must be tight with the arms held in an overhead position.

There are usually two ways to use whip backs in a series. The easiest to learn is alternations or alternate back flips. In alternates, a flip-flop is done between each back

ON TAKEOFF, THE feet should be in front of the body for proper lift.

flip with all flips except the last being whip backs. The middle whip backs are a little below shoulder height and resemble a high, fast flip-flop without hands.

Bounding back flips are a little higher than alternates, with the body rotating at shoulder height and the takeoff position a little closer to vertical.

The rebound necessary to complete whip backs is often misunderstood by young tumblers. They will often bend their knees 90 degrees or more, thinking they can jump through the stunt. Too much bend in the knees or arms usually works against the tumbler. Instead of adding power, the tumbler loses it because the bent limb acts like a "cushion" that absorbs power and speed. A good example would be to com-pare the bounce of a fully inflated with a partially deflated basketball. Obviously the deflated ball will not bounce as high because it "gives" and cushions the force. Bending the knees too much cushions a tumbler's rebound in much the same manner.

FORWARD SOMERSAULTS

In the forward somersault it is much more difficult to produce rotation, making it harder than the back flip. Although more difficult to master, the stunt is far less dangerous than learning a back flip. The problem in learning this skill, as in all somersaults, is to attain maximum lift while maintaining spin.

There are three different ways to use the arms for lift in front-flips. Each technique has advantages for different tumbling situations. We will use the overhand lift first because it is the most commonly used technique during tumbling routines; it is also easier to learn.

During a front-flip you must first attain proper lift. During the lead-up run the arms are at the sides moving normally. At the beginning of the hurdle step, begin to raise the arms up together. At the point of contact after the hurdle, both arms are above the shoulders and extend up as the body rebounds after the hurdle. The feet are slightly ahead of the body to "block" for maximum height. As you lift from the fully extended arm in an upward direction, keep the head neutral and raise the hips up behind to initiate flip. After you begin to flip, accelerate the action by ducking the head toward the knees and grab a tuck.

For a full one-half of front flips, the tumbler's vision is obscured by his legs. At that point many tumblers will release the tuck too early for the landing. Hang on to the tuck long enough to land on your feet with enough forward momentum to continue down the mats.

As mentioned above, the biggest problem to overcome in learning front flips is tucking the head and shoulders too soon. Luckily there are three lift methods to choose from. They are: the overhead lift, the Russian lift, and the underhand lift.

The overhand lift described above is usually easier. It is also used when working into and out of front flips.

The Russian lift uses a circular arm motion that produces a rear arm lift and probably a little more hip lift or somersault.

The underhand lift, like the Russian lift, is only effective on the front flip immediately after a preliminary run. With the underhand lift a tumbler can run faster because the hands stay near the sides all the way through the hurdle step. After the hur-

dle, the arms quickly circle and lift forward, then upward to complete the flip. When this method is employed, the additional forward momentum makes it easy to work into another skill.

In all front flips it is very important that the takeoff angle be very close to vertical, with the feet slightly in front of the body. It is not unusual to see young tumblers cover as much as 10 feet horizontally down the mats during a front flip. They are so concerned about getting around during the flip that they lean forward on takeoff. For every extra foot a tumbler travels laterally, height is sacrificed.

Working Into and Out of Front Somersaults

The best sequence to use for working into front-flips is the front handspring front-flip. Front handsprings are usually learned with a preliminary run. If the tumbler can execute a stretched, running front handspring to an immediate rebound jump, he is ready to work into a front-flip. The landing position of the handspring should be nearly vertical, with the feet slightly in front of the body and the arms overhead. After blocking off the mat, keep your arms up and head neutral until after the hips begin to flip up. If you rush the front flip by dropping the head too soon, the trick will be low, too long, or unfinished. It is best to use only an overhead lift when working into front somersaults.

A good training drill for front tumbling is to perform a handspring front-flip from a standing position. This will force the tumbler to develop good techniques because he will not be able to rely on the preliminary run for power. After practicing several standing drills, the front tumbling sequence seems almost effortless with a lead-up run. The tumbler who can perform the standing drill will also build confidence that will carry over to competition situations. This type of training is similar to the

WHEN PERFORMING TRAINING drills, concentrate on technique rather than power.

overtraining methods used in weight lifting or track. If you practice with heavier weights, run longer distances, or tumble without a run, you are training your body to perform under difficult circumstances. Then, on the day of competition, you will compete in a situation that requires less energy than an everyday practice. Your performance should be easier in your mind, therefore increasing confidence and giving you an edge over the field.

A correctly executed series of front tumbling tricks will feel overflipped or overrotated until you get used to it. In order to work out of a front-flip into a handspring, you must overflip and land on one leg, immediately preparing for the next handspring.

Front alternations can be performed with either handsprings or headsprings in between the front somersaults.

When you work into and out of front somys with front handsprings, you must use a walk-out after each flip, because the handspring requires a one-foot takeoff.

"Alternates" with headsprings require a two-foot takeoff and two-foot landing for all front-flips and headsprings in the sequence.

DOUBLE SOMERSAULTS

Double somersaults, forward and backward, are advanced stunts that should be attempted only by expert tumblers. Before attempting a double flip you should be able to raise your body (measure at the hips) a minimum of one or two feet above head height while executing a back flip. This "power tumbling" that produces great lift must be consistent or your attempt at performing a double flip will be far too dangerous.

The safest method to learn double flips is to use a trampoline and overhead spotting rig. On a trampoline the student will be able to bounce much higher than on the floor; this will give him more time in the air to perform. The use of a spotting belt will insure complete safety, thus allowing the student to concentrate on proper technique.

In learning this skill many problems must be solved, one of which is how to develop enough rotation and height to complete two somersaults in the air. The basic rules for doubles are the same as for single flips. The arms, upper body, head, and takeoff angle determine the height and trajectory of the trick. The flip must be initiated with the lower body. The difference between singles and doubles is the greater height requirement in turning over twice. The height factor is influenced by the speed and the angle of taking off.

It is clear that a large circle will spin slower than a smaller circle if the same force is used to spin both circles. Also if a large circle is spun and then is suddenly *reduced* in diameter, it will spin faster. This is the technique used by figure skaters in a "scratch spin." The skater begins the spin with the arms extended and speeds up the rotation by pulling in the arms. In tumbling, instead of using the arms as the end points of a circle, the and legs are the opposite ends of a circle.

As the tumbler leaves the ound with the arms up, the first quarter the initial somersault is performed in an open position. After height and spin have been established, the tumbler accelerates the flipping action by pulling his knees in tight, shortening his "flipping diameter."

It is very important not to grab the tuck too early. You must first show a body position stretched upward to gain height and to help you eventually move into a tight tuck position. You must not reach the hands downward or forward to the knees during double backs. Since all lift and flip must be up and back, reaching down or forward for the knees would be counterproductive and would hamper the execution of this trick.

After the tumbler has mastered double flips on the trampoline, the next step is to attempt the stunt in an overhead rig on the floor. Again the student will be able to experience the complete sequence without fear of injury.

There are two extremely important concepts the athlete must be aware of when moving this skill to the floor. They both seem to violate all previously taught tumbling and trampoline principles. When blocking before most back flips you are instructed on the flip-flops to move the feet as close to the hands as possible. On the double back, the second phase of the flip-flop should produce a block with the feet striking the mat well to the rear of the hands. If this elongated block is not used, the tumbler will prematurely rotate at such great speed that grabbing a tuck will be almost impossible. This double back is not only different from most tricks at its origin but is also finished in a unique manner. When coming out of a tuck position in most stunts, you open your tuck on a 45-degree angle to the floor and use visual guidance to bring your legs forward to a vertical position. In opening a double back, there is no visual contact and the opening is directly downward; the tuck is never released early.

The next step would be to perform the double with one or two coaches actively spotting the entire movement and with a crash pad for a safe landing.

An expert tumbler can eventually perform the double without an active spot by the coach, using crash pads or landing mats to make repeated landings easier.

There is another method for learning double flips that doesn't rely on belts or spotters. In this method, multiple crash pads are piled up four or five feet high.

The tumbler performs high punch flips

into the mats, adding more and more rotation until he completes 1¼ flips before hitting the mats. Then all but one or two mats are taken away and the tumbler repeats the high 1¼ flip. He hangs on to the tuck, completing two flips.

This method reportedly has been used with great success by the Japanese Olympic Team. It requires much more time to learn, but produces excellent results. According to many coaches, double flips require one or two years to master safely.

NEVER PERFORM THE double without proper coaching and spotting.

A FULL TWISTING backward somersault.

chapter 5
TWISTING

By the time tumblers reach an advanced level, they will combine twisting and somersault movements. Twisting can be defined as rotation around an axis that extends vertically from head to feet (as opposed to flipping around the horizontal axis from one hip to the other). In all judging systems, the twisting somersault is considered difficult and is rewarded accordingly.

Some of the most impressive and beautiful movements in tumbling are multiple twisting flips. During a twist, the tumbler holds his body in a lay-out position with his legs straight and toes pointed. This is more aesthetically pleasing to most people than the tuck position as held in a double back.

The trampoline is an excellent teaching aid on which beginning students can learn twisting tricks. The authors have had success using the trampoline in conjunction with overhead twisting belts or hand-spotting to teach twisting. On the trampo-

line, tumblers will attain more height and, therefore, have more time in the air to learn how to twist and flip.

In all twisting tricks there are three basic rules that must be followed: 1) For the body to twist smoothly, the tumbler must stay in the stretched position, with the arms drawn into the body; 2) All good twisting is initiated with the shoulders and arms—the rest of the body including the head follows the action started in the shoulders; 3) In every twisting somersault, the athlete must mentally start the lay-out somersault before the twist.

It is not unusual to see novice "twisters" try to twist immediately off the mat. Nine times out of ten this kind of technique is unsuccessful. The tumbler is so worried about completing the twist that he completely forgets about the somersault.

Twist must be initiated with the shoulders because the distance between the shoulders is the widest diameter of the body.

THE STUDENT SHOULD choose his or her *natural* twisting direction by doing a jump pirouette—without any prompting from the coach.

The diameter of the head is much smaller than that of the shoulders. It follows that twisting the head (smaller diameter) in order to twist the body (larger diameter) is inefficient. But, if you start to twist with the shoulders, the entire body (including the head) will follow. For the body to follow the twist of the shoulders, you must maintain a muscular tightness. Otherwise, different body parts will be twisting at different rates.

Rule three, which states that the flip must be mentally initiated before the twist, is the hardest twisting concept for students to understand. They invariably try to twist right off the mats, completely ignoring the somersault. You must concentrate on starting the flip *before* you consciously start to twist. Otherwise, there will not be enough flip to finish the trick, and the twisting will be out of alignment.

Twisting somersaults are another classic example of how actual technique differs greatly from the "feel" of the trick. As you may notice in the pictures, the tumbler seems to be twisting before he has initiated the flip. Keep in mind, however, that:

1) Quite a bit of somersault is "built

into" the round-off, flip-flop, "punch" sequence;

2) The tumbler actually feels the flip first in a correctly executed full twist.

After you understand our three basic rules for twisting, the next step is to discover which direction you will use to twist. Simply stand on the mat or trampoline and jump high, executing a full twist or pirouette. The direction you choose, without prompting, is your natural twisting direction. All twisting tricks, both forward and backward, should be taught using the same direction for twist.

Coaches should not teach a baranie by using a knee round-off on trampoline. The round-off twist direction is dependent upon the power leg (see chapter 3). It is quite common for a tumbler's round-off and natural twisting direction to be in opposite directions. Therefore, if you teach back twisting using natural twist and front twisting using opposite twist, it can be very confusing to the tumbler. The tumbler's orientation is even more difficult if the student tries to learn a trick that incorporates both back and front twisting like a half-in, half-out fliffis. In that case, you are asking the ·

tumbler to half twist in one direction and then stop that action and half twist in the other direction.

A simple test to determine if your front and back twisting are compatible is to have someone stand on your left side while you perform front and back twisting flips. If the observer sees the stomach first on the back twist, he should also see the stomach first on the front twist. If this is not the case, the tumbler is twisting in two different directions and should be corrected.

Why should twist be compatible? In the heat of competition, athletes rely on natural and learned reflexes. It is very easy to get confused if your twist is not completely natural. A moment of confusion or disorientation in the middle of a difficult twisting somersault could lead to a serious injury.

TEACHING BACK TWISTING

As we have already mentioned, most tumblers will try to twist before initiating any flip action when learning a full twisting back flip. Therefore, the progressions we will use for the "full" will emphasize the technique of mentally blocking for the back before conscious twisting action is instituted.

BACK DROP, FULL TWIST PROGRESSION

The first step in this progression is to teach the tumbler a straight body back drop on trampoline. At the moment of contact with the trampoline, the legs will be very slightly piked so that they are off the bed of the trampoline. It is very important that the student lift first the arms and then the feet when performing the back drop.

In step two, the student will perform a back drop with a full twist. Again he must lift the arms and then the feet before initiating the full twist. If the tumbler lands with his legs or body out of alignment with the length of the trampoline, he has twisted too soon. This must be practiced until it can be

performed correctly nine out of ten times.

For the third step, the tumbler puts on a twisting belt attached to an overhead spotting rig. The coach instructs the tumbler to perform a *high* full twisting back drop, with his feet almost pointing to the ceiling before he twists. If the student performs the movement correctly (lifts arms and legs first), the coach pulls on the ropes as the twist is half finished. This pull on the ropes will cause the tumbler to complete the "full twist" almost effortlessly.

It has been our experience that it is better if the coach does not explain what will take place in the last step. This way the student concentrates on lifting and flipping before twisting. Immediately after the first surprise "full," an explanation of what took place and then more repetitions of the sequence should follow.

With a coordinated athlete, it is possible to teach a full, from scratch to a safe performance, without the belt in one hour. Of course, not everyone can learn that fast, but we have had such success often enough to swear by this method.

FLOOR PROGRESSION

If you don't have an overhead spotting rig, it is possible to use the same progression using "active hand spotting."

The second progression for teaching a full is similar except that you don't use a trampoline. In step one, the student jumps into a back drop on the coach's arms, using the proper technique. In step two, the full twist back drop is also performed into the coach's arms. For step three, the coach gives the same instructions and actively spots the full, providing lift and twist.

This spotting method is obviously easier when used with smaller or younger gymnasts. However, if you have the opportunity to use it often enough and if you are strong enough, it may be used with fully developed tumblers.

IN THE SECOND photo, the tumbler's feet are being driven up and behind (according to the physical laws of action-and-reaction). Therefore, you must consciously pull your feet up in front before initiating any twist.

When the tumbler is ready to take the full and incorporate it into a tumbling series, there are two different methods of actively spotting. In the first method the spotter stands away from the direction of the twist, lifting and twisting the gymnast throughout the move. In the second method the spotter stands on the side that the tumbler will be twisting to. The spotter extends his arm toward the performer during the first half twist to keep the performer's body up. The spotter then reaches around and aids the second half twist and landing.

In summary, the following procedures should be followed by a tumbler in executing a full. He should "block" the flip-flop and attempt to gain maximum height keeping his head in a neutral position. Next, if he is twisting to his right, his left arm should be forced across his right shoulder, which will initiate a twisting action in the upper girdle. The right arm should be tucked closely into the body. The head should not be thrown back but should be in a neutral position, and it should turn in the direction of the twist.

DOUBLE AND TRIPLE TWISTING BACK FLIPS

Double and triple fulls should be learned using the same general progressions as we advocated in learning the full twist. The first step is simply changed to a double or triple twisting back drop. Then, using an overhead twisting mechanic, have a good spotter put you through the final step, making sure you lift the arms and feet up before initiating twist.

The only real difference between single and multiple twisting flips is the time you are in flight. In order to complete a double twister, you must get higher; it is quite obvious that if you do not slow down your somersaulting action, you will overturn. It

THE TAKEOFF ANGLE must be vertical, with enough somersault to perform the trick in an open position.

is not unusual to see inexperienced tumblers overflip multiple twisting somersaults.

On multi-twisting flips increasing the spin along the vertical axis is mandatory; at the same time, the rotation around the horizontal axis must be decreased. To slow backward rotation, the head should be forced forward and down onto the shoulder. The arm opposite the direction of your twist should wrap across the front of the body at chest height instead of over the shoulder. This wrapping action of the arm must also be more explosive to ensure greater twisting action.

HALF TWISTS, ONE-AND-A-HALF TWISTS, TWO-AND-A-HALF TWISTS

We have purposely left the half twist and multiple half twist until after the full twist.

It is our feeling that the technique of teaching a half twist flip first and then a half plus a half for a "full" twist is a mistake. If a tumbler becomes accustomed to thinking of a "full" as two halves, it may be very difficult to teach a double (and also difficult to perfect the full twist).

Half twisting somersaults are relatively simple to learn. The student merely has to perform an open back flip and then turn the shoulders and head to the rear. The value of halves and multiple twists ending with a half is their use in the middle of a series of tricks. In fact, a half or one-and-a-half to a one-foot landing (or step out) immediately into a round-off back handspring can be advantageous when one is constructing routines.

FRONT TWISTING

DURING THE ONE-FOOT takeoff, initial somersault is provided by the back leg.

The general rules we stated for back twisting apply also to front twisting. It is, however, much more difficult to initiate forward flip before twist. The reason for this is the way the human body is put together. It is easy to bend forward at the waist because there are many large muscles designed to promote this action. Therefore, if you are trying to flip forward, you will have a tendency to bend forward too soon; this action reduces your height.

To overcome the error of bending forward too quickly, drills should be devised that emphasize an extended body lift. It is also important to incorporate a strong heel-lifting action. Perhaps, you could

place crash mats one on top of another until they are chest high. Now, in order for a tumbler to turn a front flip and land on top of this platform, upper lift will be essential. This will also acquaint the tumbler with the "heel drive" necessary for front twisting.

There are other differences between front and back twisting. Most back twisting uses complete twists (single, doubles, etc.). Most front twisting tricks end on the half twists. It is easier to land front twisting tricks that end on the half twist rather than on a full twist, because this enables the tumbler to view his landing surface.

The correct sequence for teaching front twisting begins with the baranie or half twisting front somersault. Like the back full twist, it is easier to teach the baranie on trampoline.

Have the tumbler land on his knees; then drive his feet up so that he lands in a handstand. In step two, add more force so the legs will continue over while he keeps his eyes on the mat. After completing the half twist, he should land on his knees (be sure that the twist is compatible). After the tumbler can perform this without a stop, he should try to finish landing on his feet. Then he should try it from feet to feet, finally performing the whole trick without touching his hands.

Before adding twist to the baranie for a full twisting or one-and-one-half twisting front, you must be able to perform the baranie with sufficient heel drive to finish the trick in an open position.

When you take your front twisting tricks to the floor, it is possible to perform the baranie without a lead-up trick. Baranies can

be performed with either a one or two-foot takeoff. All other tricks (full twisting front, one-and-one-half twisting front, etc.) are performed out of front handsprings on tinsicas.

Except for one more major conceptual difference between front and back twisting, the basic principles of back twisters can be applied while you turn over in a forward direction. This last difference is in the body position. All back twisting is performed while the body is in a laid-out position; front twisting uses a body that is in a slight pike configuration.

The time required to teach a tumbler to twist varies greatly among athletes. For some, the idea of twisting is easy to comprehend, and twisting is a very natural movement. For others it is alien and may require weeks, months, or even years to perfect. There is no tumbling skill where this variation in learning rate on the part of the student is as great.

AN AERIAL CARTWHEEL, showing the proper angle between the takeoff foot and the center of gravity.

chapter 6
AERIALS

The last category of tumbling moves is aerials. Aerial cartwheels and walkovers are not a part of normal power tumbling. They are used extensively in women's floor exercise routines and, for variety, men have recently begun to incorporate these moves into their routines.

To understand and have success in attempting any form of an aerial, a few basic concepts must be learned. The first concept is that of the law of motion: a body in motion will tend to stay in motion, and a body at rest will stay at rest unless acted upon by an outside force.

We are concerned with the concept that a body in motion will continue to move. This is very important in understanding the blocking action that would lead to a correctly performed aerial. A gymnast moving in a linear direction will continue to do so unless he creates a vertical force to redirect his path of movement upward. For such an occurrence to take place, the gymnast must reach forward with his legs prior to his last contact with the tumbling mat and he must execute a forceful push in the forward-downward direction.

This blocking action will result in a rise of the center of the body's mass at a predetermined angle. The direction and size of this angle will be dependent upon the amount of force involved and the angle at which it is applied.

In aerial work, the last step forward should be low and quick, and the gymnast should exert a push in a forward-downward direction with a slight lean backward from the shoulders. This is basic biomechanics.

The second concept is that of the law of action-reaction: for every action there is an equal and opposite reaction. In terms of understanding blocking and parallelogram forces, we need only be reminded of the fact that when walking down the street, one employs this law; by exerting a force with the

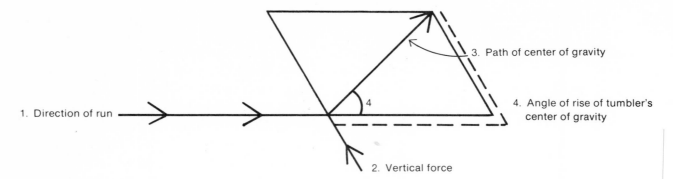

1. Direction of run

2. Vertical force

3. Path of center of gravity

4. Angle of rise of tumbler's center of gravity

leg down upon the ground, the opposite and equal force permits us to move.

In aerial work, the last step or block off the tumbling mat should be a push, which will result in a force opposite to the direction in which the push was exerted.

Before attempting aerials the gymnast should work on dive cartwheels. In the dive cartwheel, the gymnast should try to place his lead leg further in front of the body in an effort to force his mass up and over the power leg.

When the gymnast can perform a dive cartwheel from a stand and cover some distance in the air, he is ready for the next step—the aerial itself. Use only a few running steps (four maximum), reach out with the takeoff leg, blocking quickly upon takeoff. Drive the back leg up and around with much force, similar to that of a front handspring. Keep the chest up, not permitting the shoulder to lean forward over the lead leg upon takeoff. Allow the head to look forward, never dropping the head down. The arms can throw back or in a Russian or reverse lift or can be lifted forward and upward. At the same time, lift the upper torso up; inhale throughout the aerial.

The entire body will appear to rise during the rotational phase and appear to be momentarily suspended in the air. Continue to drive the lead leg up forward and downward until good contact with the mat is made. Upon landing, the upper torso should be tight, keeping the rib-cage high and erect, the head in alignment with the body and looking forward. The entire landing should be soft and continuous, with the landing leg forced under the body.

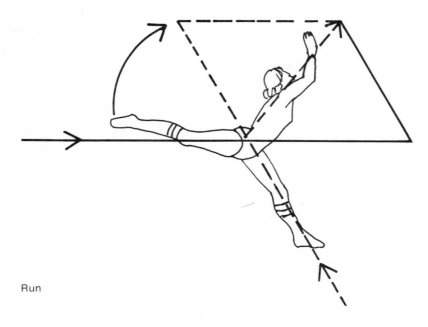

Run

Some of the most common mistakes would be the employment of too many steps in preparation of the stunt in an ineffective block. This will give the aerial the appearance of being low and heavy, barely getting around.

Allowing the shoulder to lean forward in front of the lead leg is another common error. This will result in an ineffective block, also giving the aerial the appearance of being low and heavy, barely getting an adequate rotation.

Another mistake is not driving the back leg effectively upward. This will not allow the body to rotate efficiently.

Think in terms of allowing the heel to rise rapidly and to be the leading force in the kick. If a person persists in dropping his head and shoulders down upon the initial block of the lead leg, an active form of spotting can be incorporated. The spotter should stand on the side of the lead leg and with the hand closest to the gymnast, palm up and outstretched, place his hand on the gymnast's shoulder, keeping it in place at approximately hip level. This will prevent the gymnast from leaning forward in front of the lead leg. It will also help create the desired blocking angle of approximately 90 degrees.

There are also many mechanical aids that can be employed when learning aerials. A takeoff board can be used to help beginners gain greater block which, of course, will result in more height. Any of the commercially produced boards are sufficient to serve in this capacity, or you can make an inclined plane from scrap wood.

A sash can be used for spotting aerial cartwheels. A sash can be made from any piece of material three to four feet in length that is sufficiently strong to hold the performer. You simply place it around his waist, bringing both ends together in your hand. If he blocks with his right leg, stand to his right; reverse your position if he is left legged. This cloth spotting supplement will be an excellent help in lifting the tumbler through this skill. The aerial walkover can be taught using the traditional hand or overhead belt.

Until now we have not pointed out technical differences between the aerial walkover and cartwheel. Although they appear to be radically different, the principles we have stated can be applied to both of these skills. The major difference is not in the takeoff or landing but in the body position in flight. In the aerial walkover the back is hyperextended; in the cartwheel the leg is piked under on landing. Without great back flexibility, it is virtually impossible to execute an aerial walkover. The tumbler must consciously endeavor to maintain this arched position throughout the trick. This arched back concept is further emphasized by the attempt to force the landing leg under the body.

Although aerials are not an important part of a power tumbling routine, their versatility in other areas makes them a part of a tumbling program.

PROPER WARM-UPS WILL lengthen your tumbling career by preventing injuries.

chapter 7
WARM-UPS

A good warm-up before workouts is an absolute necessity for every athlete. A warm-up prepares the body for strenuous activity and will help prevent injuries. It accomplishes this by increasing the efficiency of muscular contractions and by speeding up the flow of electrical impulses through the nervous system. The rate of chemical changes is also increased, along with a 20 percent increase in general flexibility.

The human body at rest or in normal activity functions at a level that does not place stress on the muscles or cardiovascular system. The majority of the blood is pooled or stored in the organs of the abdomen. Large portions of the capillary systems in the skeletal muscles are closed, restricting the flow of blood. The heart beats approximately 72 times per minute, and the breathing is relaxed and moderately shallow.

During exercise the capillaries in the muscles open up, and nearly 55 percent of the blood flows to the muscles. Breathing also becomes deeper and faster.

The reason for these changes lies in the chemistry of muscular contraction. During exercise, chemicals inside the muscles change, releasing energy and producing waste products. The muscles require a dramatic increase in blood flow in order to bring in oxygen and nutrients and to flush away waste products.

If you begin heavy muscular contraction before cardiovascular adaptation has taken place, waste products will accumulate in the muscles, causing stiffness and soreness. A muscle that hasn't been warmed up functions at a low level of efficiency. Warm-up activities should include movements that increase blood flow without excessive muscular contractions.

Many individuals who fail to understand the principles of a good warm-up use resistance exercises. These resistance exercises, such as sit-ups, push-ups, leg-lifts, etc., put the muscles through contraction before sufficient blood is flowing to the muscles.

Dancers, gymnasts, and track athletes have traditionally used stretching or flexibility exercises, instead of resistance movements, for warm-ups.

Stretching exercises will increase blood flow to the muscles, preparing them for heavier exercise. In addition, the muscles are not put through heavy contraction during stretching exercises. Stretching, if performed regularly, will also increase the tumbler's flexibility, thus making it easier to perform many tumbling skills.

Before we describe a specific stretching warm-up for tumblers, there are several rules to follow concerning stretching and flexibility exercises:

I. 1) Always stretch slowly and smoothly; avoid fast bouncing or "ballistic stretching";
    2) Do not try to improve your flexibility too much, too soon—you could seriously pull or tear muscles;
    3) Stretch each area until you feel a little pain; then try to go another quarter inch;
    4) When stretching the back or spine one way, always follow with a stretch in the opposite direction (to avoid injury to spinal discs);
    5) Be organized; start at the head and work your way down to the legs.

II. Starting at the top of the body, you should stretch in the following manner: The neck followed by the chest and shoulders; wrists and forearms; waist, stomach, and lower back; the hamstrings; calf muscles; quadriceps.

The following exercises, which will stretch the seven major areas of the body, should fully prepare anyone for more rigorous activity:

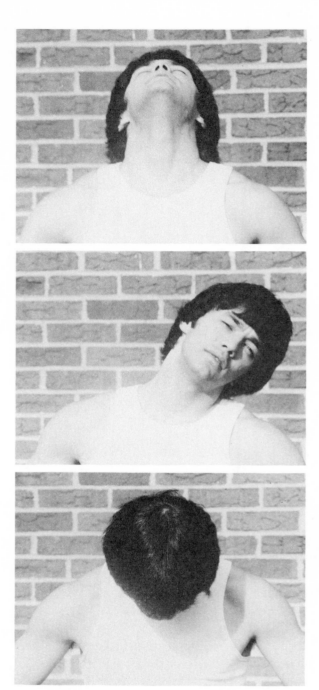

Neck: Place hands on hips, keep shoulders level and rotate the head in a circle 10-15 times; reverse the circle 10-15 times.

Chest; shoulders: Swing the arms back and forth at shoulder level and parallel to the floor. The elbows should be straight and the arms should cross in front of the body. One arm at a time, swing the arm in a wide circular movement, gradually

with feet shoulder width apart and toes pointing inward, lean forward keeping the knees and back straight and the heels on the mat.

Hamstrings; neck: Lying down on the mat, balance on shoulders, hips elevated over head; bring knees toward the mat next to head slowly; raise legs again; then bounce the legs down with the knees straight. Alternate with bent and straight legs.

Hamstrings; inner thighs: Lying on back, hips on the mat and the knees bent over chest; grab heels and straighten the legs, pulling the heels apart and downward. Sit in a wide straddle position, knees and back straight; attempt to slowly lay the upper torso onto right leg, then left leg; then place upper body on the mat between legs.

Hamstrings; quadriceps: In a hurdler's stretch, use the technique we have just

increasing the speed; reverse the circle; switch arms and repeat.

Wrists; forearms: With both arms extended in front and elbows straight, contract the hands backward, fingers wide apart; then flex the hands downward, fingers curled together; repeat five times each way; then shake hands vigorously.

Waist; lower back: Clasp hands overhead, elbows straight; lean slowly from one side to the other, keeping the arms and legs straight. Place hands on hips; circle from the waist 5-10 times; reverse the direction 5-10 times.

Hamstrings: Feet together, knees bent slightly, bend forward from the waist, touching hands to the mat; straighten one leg, then the other, then both without moving the hands.

Calves; hamstrings: Facing and standing about two to three feet from a wall

EXERCISES FOR THE waist and lower back.

IT IS IMPORTANT to warm up thoroughly the hamstrings and calves before tumbling.

described and stretch toward the straight leg; then lie down on back as bent knee rises off the mat. In a slow, rhythmic motion, attempt to force the knee back down to the mat; repeat on the opposite side.

Calf; hamstrings: Sitting with legs together, bent, and perpendicular to the floor, grab the feet over the toes; attempt to straighten legs while pulling the feet back and body down.

Lower back: Lying on back, place hands on the mat next to head, fingers extended to the front; bend the knees, placing the feet on the floor; push up into a back bend.

(Opposite) Lower back: Roll back on shoulders, elevating hips overhead; try to rest the knees on the mat to the side of or behind head.

Shoulders; chest: From a sitting position, reach to the rear with both hands, arms straight. Raise the hips and bend the knees, rocking forward and increasing the angle between the arms and the body.

As we mentioned in Chapter 3, fundamental tricks and combinations should be

BE SURE TO keep your heels on the floor.

incorporated into the warm-up on a regular basis. Immediately after the above stretches, the tumbler should add a five-minute to fifteen-minute tumbling session that uses the fundamentals. Start with forward rolls, proceed through cartwheels and handsprings, and eventually end with flip-flop back flips from a stand.

The entire warm-up will last from 15 to 30 minutes. At the end of that period, the tumblers should be able to perform any trick with a reduced fear of injury or stiffness. The warm-up should never be overlooked or minimized. Should an emergency situation arise—such as arriving to a meet late—a quick warm-up would consist of one lower back exercise, one hamstring exercise, and one calf exercise, followed by some slow running or jogging in place. Use this abbreviated warm-up only in emergency situations.

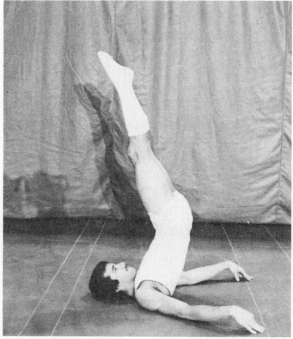

1

START THE MOVEMENT slowly to avoid a pulled muscle.

2

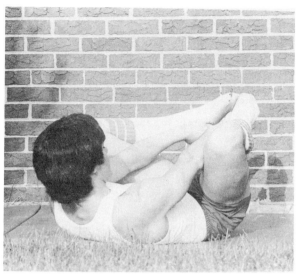

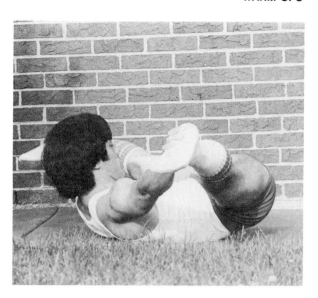

KEEP THE HIPS down on the mat during this stretch.

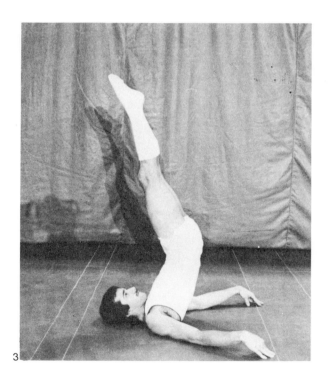

3

4

3

FOR MAXIMUM RESULTS, you must keep your knees straight.

3

IF YOU HAVE knee problems, be very careful with this exercise.

3

TRY TO PLACE your stomach on your legs with your knees straight.

AFTER EVERY BACKBEND, you should flex your back the other way to protect your spine.

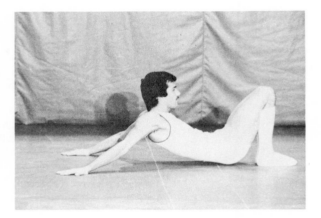

KEEP YOUR ARMS straight throughout this exercise.

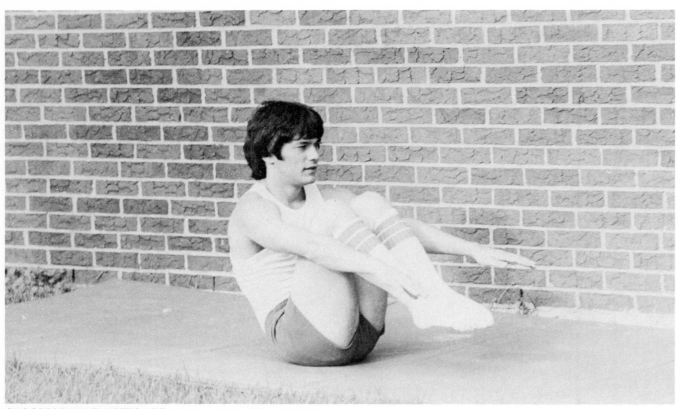
SUCCESSFUL ATHLETES ARE always well-conditioned athletes.

chapter 8
CONDITIONING

Tumbling is an excellent developmental activity for young children. Tumblers must use every muscle group in the body in addition to moving most joints through a large range of motion. If young students take proper warm-ups and use good equipment, tumbling can be a safe and enjoyable way to achieve physical fitness.

Competitive tumbling requires strength and endurance like any other amateur or professional sport. As all competitive athletes know, if you want to have an edge over the competition, you must start with two components: good fundamentals and superior physical conditioning.

If a student begins a sport like tumbling already in good condition, he will learn faster than someone in poor shape. However, as you prepare for competition, it is necessary to add specific exercises for muscle groups important to tumbling.

In Europe it is very common to see athletes break down their activities into component parts and condition themselves with these simpler movements. For example, a long jumper who takes off on his right leg might carry a weight on his back and hop repeatedly on the right leg. After a period of such conditioning, the actual jump will improve dramatically. In addition, each single jump will seem to require less effort—making long competitions a little easier.

Another important component of conditioning should be endurance training. When you are required to play ball for long periods, run for time, or tumble three or four times in two minutes, endurance or staying power is important.

Our conditioning exercise will be of three types: (1) exercises aimed at muscle groups important for tumbling; (2) exercises that

MILITARY PRESS TO full extension.

are repetitions of tumbling movements (reduced to component parts); and (3) endurance exercises aimed at improving cardio-respiratory endurance.

The exercises should be performed in the exact order that we present them. Don't gang up on one muscle group with three or four successive exercises. Allow the muscle to recuperate while you exercise a different area.

The cardiovascular or endurance exercises should be performed last; they will be more effective then. All conditioning should be performed after the actual tumbling workout, or several hours before the tumbling (so as to allow recovery time).

Wrists: (1) Wrist curls. Holding a barbell with weights, arms on knees; curl the hands all the way up and down; 7-10/set, 1-3 sets/day.

Triceps, deltoids: (2) Military press (to full extension). Starting with the bar on the chest, press all the way overhead until

the elbows are straight and the shoulders touch the ears; 7-10/set, 1-3 sets/day.

Abdomen: (3) "V"-sit-ups. On the back, hands next to body; keeping knees straight, raise legs and shoulders off the mat simultaneously, trying to touch toes with hands; then return to reclining position; 10-15/set, 1-3 sets/day.

Quadriceps: (4) Half knee bends to heel raises. With the barbell and weights on shoulders, bend the knees only half-way (90 degrees); then straighten the legs and raise all the way up on the toes; 7-10/set, 1-3 sets/day.

Abdomen: (5) Bent knee sits. Lie on back with knees straight, arms at the side; simultaneously raise the body up and bend the legs up, trying to touch the knees and chest together; 7-10/set, 1-3 sets/day.

Triceps: (6) Handstand push-ups. In the handstand position against the wall, bend the arms and try to touch the nose to the mat; then push back up to handstand position; 7-10/set, 1-3 sets/day.

Lower back: (7) Inch-worm. With knees straight, bend forward at the waist; place the hands on the floor six to twelve inches in front of the feet; try to raise the hips and pull the feet to the hands, moving down the mat; 7-10/set, 1-3 sets/day.

Quadriceps, calves: (8) Blocking drill.

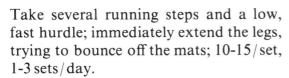

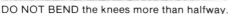

DO NOT BEND the knees more than halfway.

Take several running steps and a low, fast hurdle; immediately extend the legs, trying to bounce off the mats; 10-15/set, 1-3 sets/day.

Deltoids: (9) Handstand shoulder shrugs. In a handstand position and keeping the arms straight, lift the body up and down by extending and shrugging the shoulders; 7-10/set, 1-3 sets/day.

Abdomen: (10) Straight-leg raises. Hanging from a bar, raise the legs up to the bar and down again, keeping the knees straight; 7-10/set, 1-3 sets/day.

Heart, lungs, endurance: (11) Cardiovascular drills.* (A) Rope skipping. Jump rope, alternating between one- and two-leg jumps; stay on the toes; do not

---

*If you have never worked on cardiovascular drills, do not overstrain yourself at first. If you begin to feel dizzy or sick, *slow down*—even if it means going slower than our suggested pace. You must work up to the pace listed gradually and consistently.

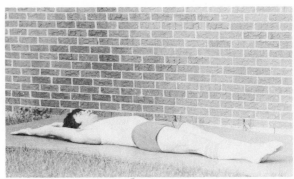 

IN THE BEGINNING of the exercise, try to keep the lower back pressed against the mat.

exceed three minutes per set; 3-5 sets/day.

(B) Bicycling. Ride at least five miles in one sitting, keeping a pace of at least 30-50 revolutions (of the pedals) per minute.

(C) Running. Try to run at least 1.5 miles without stopping, keeping a pace of eight minutes per mile or better.

For all of the conditioning exercises, you should start with light weights and low repetitions per set. Generally it is best to perform the strengthening exercises every other day or three times per week.

After you have increased your level of conditioning, you may perform one exercise for each muscle group every day (except for exercises with weights). Every other day have a harder session by adding the weight exercises. As your strength increases, add three to five pounds to the weights every ten days or when you can lift the previous weight more often than the prescribed total.

The only conditioning exercises we recommend you perform every day, or at least six out of seven days, are the cardiovascular drills. Given equal coordination, training, and age, the better conditioned between any two athletes will have the edge in any competition.

DON'T CHEAT: USE your back and not your legs.

THE ARMS SHOULD remain straight during this exercise.

TO AVOID "SHIN-SPLINTS" always run on a soft surface and wear proper shoes.

A TUMBLER EXHIBITING good form will always show pointed toes whenever the feet leave the ground.

chapter 9
JUDGING AND EVALUATION

Tumbling has been considered part of the overall gymnastic program for many years. Therefore, the application of the same officiating rules governing both tumbling and gymnastics was a natural phenomenon. It soon became obvious, however, that there were many difficulties in attempting to apply gymnastic rules to the sport of tumbling. Throughout the 1930s, '40s, '50s, and '60s, many rule modifications were inaugurated. Because they were tied so closely to the officiating of apparatus events, none were successful. During the '70s a system was advanced by the United States Trampoline and Tumbling Association that is used throughout the world.

Because of the radical departure from tradition, some experienced judges at first may resist using this system. I feel, however, that if they judge under these rules for a short period of time, they will not only completely accept them, but they will realize their greater objectivity in determining the winning performance.

The 1970s appear to be an era of great change in the officiating of tumbling. Although not nearly as widely used as the F. I. T. rules, the Muczyzko system has been employed in the James Rozanas National Invitational Tumbling Tournament for the past three years. It is also used in many age group meets in the Chicago area and is in the process of being reviewed as to its applicability for use in the Illinois High School System. Mr. Muczyzko has given us permission to incorporate his work into this publication.

This new system is both easy to understand and easy to apply. No major retraining of judges is needed since the basic concepts of difficulty, combination, execution, and bonus points (ROV) have been preserved. The internal accounting, however, has been changed, and that's the difference.

The system is most easily described by considering the major point-awarding categories of difficulty, combination, execution, and bonus points.

DIFFICULTY—count only the 10 highest value parts:

$$C = .4$$
$$B = .3$$
$$A = .1$$

The maximum is .4(10) = 4.

COMBINATION—deductions or additions are as follows:

Bounders	.2
Alternations	.2
Twisting (full twist minimum)	.2
Front or Side Work (3 moves minimum)	.6
Spiritual Expression*	.2
TOTAL	1.4

EXECUTION-the standard deductions can apply. The maximum is *10.0*. Also if fewer than 10 parts are shown, the execution maximum is:

10 parts	4.0
9 parts	3.6
8 parts	3.2
7 parts	2.8
6 parts	2.4
5 parts	2.0
4 parts	1.6
3 parts	1.2
2 parts	.8
1 part	.4

*This deduction or addition is used when faults are observed wherein no format deduction is listed, *e.g.,* too many A's, too many moves of one type, general impression.

No mitigation is used. If a move *other than* a round-off, flip-flop, or front handspring is used for the third time with the same preceding and succeeding parts, it loses its value, but does not count as a part of no value and no repetition deductions are made under combination. This does not include combined value moves. For example, four tuck front saltos in a row is given the value of C + C + B.

Typical execution deductions are:

(1) Poor position of feet, legs, arms, head—up to .2
(2) Stopping (each time)—.2 to .8
(3) Technical execution faults—up to .2
(4) Tumbling off the mat, per move—up to .2
(5) Lack of rhythm (slow), per pass—up to .2
(6) Lack of height (except for whip movements)—up to .2
(7) Poor landings on finishing moves—up to .4
(8) Moves of no value—.2

BONUS-ROV—Risk, Originality, Virtuosity

The maximum is .6. The usual FIG-NGJA definitions may be used here. An award .2 maximum in each category is possible. Of course you may award a total of .6 for all three categories together. Examples of risk are double backs, double twists, using few flip-flops, mixed work, etc. Examples of originality are new moves or combinations seldom seen. Virtuosity is simply excellence in form and technique, beyond minimum requirements.

In summary, the MAXIMUMS are:

Difficulty	.4(10) = 4.0
Combination	1.4
Execution	4.0
ROV	.6
TOTAL	10.0

The number of passes need not be restricted, but doing more than is required would be self-defeating, that is, more execution faults would be found. If desired, a limitation of 3 to 4 passes may be made, but 2 or even 3 passes could show risk in the bonus points category.

EXAMPLES OF USE
Consider this first elementary exercise.

(1) (A) round-off—(A) flip-flop—(B) tuck salto
(2) (B) front—(A) roll—(B) front
(3) (A) round-off—(A) flip-flop—(B) back (tuck)—(A) flip-flop—(B) back (tuck)

Difficulty	5A(.1)	=	.5
	5B(.3)	=	1.5
	TOTAL	=	2.0

Combination
Alternations	.2	= .2
Front Work	.6	= .6
TOTAL		=.0

Execution
max - deductions
4.0	-	2.0	=	2.0
ROV			=	0.0
TOTAL FINAL SCORE			=	4.8

(It is assumed that 2.0 in deductions were incurred.)

An intermediate exercise could be scored as follows:

(1) (A) round-off—(A) flip-flop—(C) full—(A) flip-flop—(C) full
(2) (B) front—(A) roll—(B) front
(3) (A) round-off—(A) flip-flop—(B) back—(A) flip-flop—(C) full

Difficulty
3 C's = 3(.4) =	1.2
3 B's = 3(.3) =	.9
4 A's = 4(.1) =	.4
	2.5

Combination

Bounders =	.2
Front Work =	.6
Twisting =	.2
Alternations	.2
	1.2
ROV =	0.0
Execution—4.0 - 1.5 =	2.5
TOTAL	6.2

Finally an advanced exercise can be scored as follows:

(1) (B) front step out—(A) round-off—(A) flip-flop—(C) back ½ twist step out—(A) round-off—(A) flip-flop—(B) back—(C) full—(A) flip-flop—(C) full
(2) (A) tinsica—(B) tigna—(A) tinsica—(C) tigna—(C) front
(3) (A) round-off—(A) flip-flop—(B) back—(A) flip-flop—(C + C) double back

Difficulty
7 C's = 7(.4) =	2.8
3 B's = 3(.3) =	.9
	3.7

Combinations
All requirements met =	1.4
ROV =	.5

Execution
Maximum deductions—4.0 - .5 =	3.4
TOTAL	8.9

CONCLUSIONS:

The proposed system has the following advantages:

(1) True difficulty awards are given. Difficulty is not emphasized, but more accurately awarded.
(2) At a later stage, if desired, the B moves may be given refined values such as:
    B = .2 example back salto tuck
    B+= .3 example back salto ½ twist
    + indicates a higher value
(3) The scores may be assessed both *subtractively* and *additively*. Additive assessments are faster for lower level ex-

ercise. The system works for all competitive levels.

(4) Combination deductions are simple and clear. They are either present or absent.

(5) There is considerable room for execution deductions; windfall awards are not given to short exercises, at all competitive levels.

(6) ROV is used as an additional means to help separate competitors.

(7) The same system may be used even if moves are reevaluated.

(8) No *major* judge retraining is needed.

(9) Each judges assesses the entire exercise, i.e. *one* judge may judge the event.

The main disadvantages as I see it are:

(1) The system is new, even though most of the old concepts are preserved. Therefore, some minimal retraining of judges is required.

(2) Overall scores will be lower than in the past.

RATINGS OF TUMBLING MOVES
"A" MOVES

1. Forward Roll
2. Back Roll
3. Front Handspring
4. Back Handspring
5. Back Handspring
6. Front Mounter
7. Cartwheel
8. Roundoff
9. Tinsica
10. Arabian Handspring
11. Front Headspring
12. Back Roll with Half Turn

"B" MOVES

1. Back Salto (Somy) Tuck, Pike, Layout, or Whipback
2. Front Salto (Somy) Tuck, or Pike or with Stepout
3. Front Salto with Half Twist
4. Baranie
5. Back Salto with Quarter Twist
6. Back Salto with Half Twist
7. Side Salto Tuck or Pike
8. Tigna
9. Arabian Back Salto
10. Aerial Walkover
11. Aerial Cartwheel

"C" MOVES

Back Salto with 1/1 Twist, Tuck, Pike, or Layout

Front Salto Layout (Hips Height of Head)

1¾ Front Salto, Tuck, or Pike

Side Salto Layout

Back Salto with ½ Twist to a Stepout

COMBINATIONS AND HIGHER VALUE MIXES

Double Back Salto—Tuck or Pike	C+C
Double Front Salto—Tuck	C+C
Double Front Salto—Pike	C+C+B
Back Salto 1½ Twists	C+A
Back Salto 2/1 Twists	C+B
Back Salto 2½ Twists	C+B+B
Back Salto 3/1 Twists	C+C
Handspring to Front Salto Pike	C
Front Salto 1/1 Twist	C+A
Front Salto 1½ Twists (Rudolf)	C+B
Front Salto 2/1 Twists	C+C
Front Salto 2½ Twists (Rudolf)	C+C+B
Double Salto with 1/1 Twist	C+C+C
Double Side Salto	C+C+B
Back 1¾ Salto with ½ Twist	C+C
Back-Front	C or BB
Back 1/1 Twist to Front	C+C
Back 2/1 Twist to Front	C+C+B
Double Front with ½ Twist	C+C+C
Back Bounders	B+B or C
Back Alternates	B+B

Alternating Back Fulls	C+C	Handspring Front (Tuck)	A+B
Bounding Back Fulls	C+C +B	Back Full-Back	C+B
Front Salto to Front Salto	C	Back-Back Full	B+C
Front-Front-Front	C+B	Front Handspring to Front Salto	
Front-Front-Front-Front	C+C +B	(Layout)—Hips Height of Head	C+B

appendix: f.i.t. tumbling rules

The Nissen Corporation, publisher of the *Official Handbook for Tumbling,* gave us permission to reproduce the following International Trampoline Federation (F. I. T.) Tumbling Rules.

A. GENERAL RULES

1. Individual Competition

   1.1 A tumbling routine shall consist of one (1) compulsory and four (4) voluntary passes with a minimum of three (3) skills in each pass.

       1.1.1 Tumbling shall be characterized by continuous, speedy, rhythmic hands to feet, feet to hands and feet to feet rotational jumping movements, without hesitations or intermediate steps. The performer shall display no contortion skills such as, limbers, front or back walkovers, handwalking or balancing.

       1.1.2 A tumbling routine shall be planned to demonstrate a variety of forward, backward and sideward skills. The routine should show good control, form execution, maintenance of height and difficulty. Tumbling passes must start from a run up to the mat and the last skill in each pass held stationary in a standing position.

   1.2 Preliminaries
   There shall be one compulsory and two voluntary passes. The order for starting will be drawn by ballot.

1.3   Finals
    1.3.1   For the finals, only the 10 best competitors from the preliminaries will take part.
    1.3.2   The competitor with the lowest preliminary score will start. In the event of ties, the starting order will be decided by a draw.
    1.3.3   There shall be 2 passes in the finals.

2. Team Competition
  2.1   A tumbling team consists of five (5) ladies or five (5) men.
  2.2   Every member of the team must perform five (5) passes.
  2.3   The score of the team member with the lowest number of points will be deleted from the team score after each pass.

3. Winners
  3.1   The winner is the competitor or the team with the highest overall number of points.
  3.2   Competitors with the same scores will be given the same place and medals will be awarded according to the regulations for World, Continental and Intercontinental Championships.

4. Passes
  4.1   The preliminary passes shall be as follows:
    4.1.1   The first pass shall be a compulsory pass consisting of five (5) skills.
    4.1.2   The second pass is a voluntary pass but must contain at least three (3) somersaults. No somersaults in this pass may twist more than 180 degrees.
    4.1.3   The third pass is a voluntary pass but must contain at least a somersault with a 360-degree twist.
  4.2   In the final competition each competitor must execute two (2) voluntary passes.
    4.2.1   The final voluntary passes must differ from one another but may be the same as any of the preliminary passes.
  4.3   All passes must contain a minimum of three (3) skills, including two (2) somersaults and end with a somersault, but with no more than two (2) identical skill combinations.
  4.4   The direction (forward, backward or sideward) of a skill shall be determined by the direction of rotation upon takeoff into the skill.
  4.5   When counting the number of somersaults in a pass, double somersaults count as two (2) somersaults. Triple somersaults count as three (3) somersaults.
  4.6   If a competitor is obviously disturbed while performing a pass (faulty equipment or external causes), the jury is called together by the superior judge and a second attempt may be allowed by a majority vote.

5. Dress for Competitors and Spotters
  5.1   Men: For each country a uniform gym shirt without sleeves, long white gym trousers or uniform shorts must be worn. Shoes may or may not be worn. If socks are worn they must be white. The decision is optional.
  5.2   Ladies: For each country a uniform leotard must be worn. Shoes may or may not be worn. The decision is optional.
  5.3   Spotters: Training suit and gym shoes.
  5.4   Any violation of these rules (5.1 and 5.2) will result in disqualifications. The superior judge makes the decision.

6. Competition Cards
  6.1   Each pass with difficulty rating must be written on the competition card. Only the

preliminary passes are handed in. Those in the finals will complete the last two (2) passes on their card prior to the finals.

6.2   The competition card must be given to the recorder at least two (2) hours before the start of the preliminary competition. Finalists must hand in their cards at least one hour before the start of the finals.

6.3   Changes from the listed skills on the card are permitted during a pass.

7. Tumbling Equipment

    7.1   It is required that a mat 20 to 27 meters in length, and 4 cm to 10 cm in thickness be required for all FIT competitions. A 10-meter running approach to the mat must be provided.

    7.2   The width of the mat shall be 120 cm to 190 cm.

    7.3   The mats must be connected so as to not separate during use.

    7.4   A springboard may be used for the first skill in each pass. The measurements of the springboard will be as follows: length 120 cm-125 cm, width 60 cm-63 cm, height 12 cm-13 cm.

    7.5   A landing mat measuring a minimum 180 cm by 360 cm by 10 cm whose composition is specified by the Technical Committee may be used for the landing of the final skill in each pass.

8. Height of the Hall

The interior height of the hall in which tumbling competitions are to take place must be at least 5 meters.

9. Safety

    9.1   The competitor may request from the superior judge his own spotter.

    9.2   The superior judge is responsible for controlling the actions of the spotters.

    9.3   The competitors must execute their passes without any external help. Whether the help of the spotter was needed or not will be decided by the superior judge. If a spotter helps the competitor, the pass will terminate at that point, and no credit shall be given for the spotted skill.

    9.4   Talking to the competitor by their own spotters during the pass is not permitted. Each time this rule is disregarded, it will result in a deduction of .3 pt. by the performance judges Nos. 1-4 at the instruction of the superior judge.

10.Score Sheets

    10.1   During all international competitions, the official score sheets of the FIT must be used.

    10.2   The original completed score sheets must be returned to the technical president of the FIT.

    10.3   Duties of the Chief Recorder

        10.3.1 Supply secretaries for the superior judge and judges.

        10.3.2 Recording the starting order of the preliminary and final passes.

        10.3.3 Recording of the scores and the degree of difficulty.

        10.3.4 Scrutiny and control of the entries on the competition cards and score sheets.

        10.3.5 Display the total score by order of the superior judge.

        10.3.6 Establishing the correct order of the final results.

11. Arbitration Jury

    11.1   The arbitration jury must decide on protests and state the protest fee before beginning of the competition.

    11.2   Composition

11.2.1	One member of the Praesidium or organizing committee	1
11.2.2	President of the Technical Committee	1
11.2.3	Superior judge	1
11.2.4	Two judges	2
11.2.5	Total	5

11.3   The arbitration jury's decision is final and must be abided by.

12.   Protests

12.1   A protest can only be handed in by an official representative of a Federation, a team manager or competitor.

12.2   A written protest with a protest fee must be handed to the superior judge immediately.

12.3   Protests have to be dealt with and the decision announced immediately after each round by the arbitration jury.

12.4   If the protest is overruled, the fee will be sent to the International Trampoline Federation (FIT). If the protest is sustained, the fee will be returned.

B. COMPETITION PROCEDURE

13.   Warming Up

13.1   Before the start of the competition, training on the competition mat at least two (2) hours must be given.

13.2   All competitors will be allowed two (2) practice passes before each round.

13.3   At World, Intercontinental and Continental Championships, a warming up on the competition mats during the competition is not allowed.

13.4   The organizer of World, Intercontinental, and Continental Championships must have at least two (2) sets of mats identical to the competition mats available in a nearby gym hall.

14.   Start of a Pass

14.1   Each competitor will start on the signal given by the superior judge.

14.2   The competitors in a preliminary tumbling competition shall be grouped in blocks of ten (10) competitors.

14.2.1   The first round of competition shall be the compulsory pass as in 4.1.1.

14.2.2   The second round of competition shall be the somersaulting pass as in 4.1.2.

14.2.3   The third round of competition shall be the twisting pass as in 4.1.3.

14.3   A competitor's pass shall be considered started once the first skill is initiated. The superior judge will make the decision.

15.   Required Positions During a Pass

15.1   In the tucked, piked, and straight position, the feet, legs, and knees must be kept together and the feet and toes pointed.

15.2   Depending on the requirements of the movement, legs and hips must either be tucked, piked or straight.

15.3   In the tucked and piked position, the upper body and thigh must at least be at an angle of 90 degrees (except in twisting somersaults).

15.4   In the tucked and piked position the hands must grasp the legs either below or behind the knees.

15.5   A layout back somersault is defined as a somersault with the body straight for at least the first 270 degrees of the somersault rotating at a minimum of shoulder height of the competitor. Decisions on this shall be made by the difficulty judges.

15.6   The positions and movements of the arms are free but where possible they must be straight.

16. Repetitions and Combination Requirements

16.1 In any voluntary passes the same somersault, with or without twists, must not be repeated more than once.

16.2 If the competitor disregards this rule the degree of difficulty of the excessively repeated somersaults, with or without twists, will not be counted.

16.3 Multiple somersaults with the same number of twists in the first, middle, and last phase of the somersault, have the same degree of difficulty. They are considered as different somersaults, and not as repetitions.

16.4 Tucked, piked, and straight somersaults are considered to be different from each other and not repetitions.

16.5 A somersault, with or without twists, shall be considered different in each pass if entered from a different skill.

17. Interruptions and Terminations of the Pass

17.1 A pass is to be considered interrupted and therefore terminated if the competitor:

17.1.1 Falls to the mat during a pass.

17.1.2 Tumbles off the side or end of the mat with any part of the body. The decision on this shall be made by the superior judge.

17.1.3 Receives help from his own spotter.

17.1.4 Takes intermediate steps or stops.

18. Scoring

18.1 Degree of Difficulty

18.1.1 The degree of difficulty for all somersaulting skills is evaluated according to the difficulty ratings.

18.1.2 All front and back handsprings, cartwheels, round-offs, and similar skills have no difficulty value, but have definite direction as skills within a pass.

18.1.3 Single somersaults

18.1.3.1 All aerials (1 foot takeoffs)	0.2
18.1.3.2 Tuck back somersaults	0.4
18.1.3.3 All tuck front somersaults and whipbacks	0.5
18.1.3.4 All somersaults done in the pike or layout position with the exception of twisting somersaults, add	0.1

18.1.3.5 Skills which are performed from previous somersaults (bounding) shall be awarded a bonus of .1 if in the same direction, and .2 if performed with a reversal of direction.

18.1.4 Twisting somersaults

18.1.4.1 Each ¼ twist up through two (2) full twists shall be worth	0.1
18.1.4.2 Each ¼ twist beyond two (2) twists shall be worth	0.2

18.1.5 Multiple somersaults

18.1.5.1 The value of the first and second somersault shall be doubled.

18.1.5.2 The value of the third somersault shall be tripled.

18.1.6 Twisting multiple somersaults

18.1.6.1 The value of the somersaults and twists within the skill shall be doubled.

18.1.7 A skill is judged successful upon the landing of the feet simultaneously with the hands.

18.1.8 From the difficulty standpoint a skill is judged according to the position of the feet upon landing.

18.1.9 The difficulty judges make all decisions regarding rule 18.1.

18.2 Method of scoring

18.2.1 All evaluation is done in tenths of a point.

18.2.2 The scores of the judges must be written independently of each other.

18.2.3 The superior judge and judges Nos. 1-4 evaluate technical execution, form, height, control, and rhythm. They write down their scores on a score sheet.

18.2.4 At a given signal by the superior judge, the scores of the judges must be shown simultaneously.

18.2.5 If any of the judges Nos. 1-4 fail to display their scores, then the average score of the other judges will be taken for the missing score. This decision will be made by the superior judge.

18.2.6 In the compulsory pass the highest and lowest scores of the judges Nos. 1-4 are cancelled, and the two middle scores are averaged, provided that the difference between the two (2) scores is not too great as per rule 18.3.

18.2.7 In the voluntary passes the highest and lowest scores of judges Nos. 1-4 are cancelled. Half the average of the remaining two (2) scores is the score for performance, provided that the difference between the two scores is not too great as per rule 18.3.

18.2.8 Each pass is scored separately and a total of performance plus difficulty is calculated for each voluntary pass. No difficulty is calculated for the compulsory pass.

18.2.9 Judges Nos. 5-6 check the execution of the compulsory pass, calculate the difficulty of the voluntary pass, and enter it on the competition cards.

18.2.10 Half the average of the two (2) middle scores of each voluntary pass is added to the total difficulty to determine the score for that pass.

18.2.11 If a pass has less than three (3) skills, the competitor shall receive a 0 for that pass.

18.2.12 The scores for each of the five (5) passes are added together and the competitor with the highest score is the winner.

18.2.13 The superior judge is responsible for determining the final score and the recorder is responsible for calculating and entering the score on the score sheet.

18.2.14 The showing of the total score is done by the recorder upon order of the superior judge.

18.2.15 Secretaries shall be assigned to the superior judge and the judges.

18.3 Difference in Evaluation

18.3.1 If the difference in the two (2) middle scores of judges Nos. 1-4 is greater than the following, then the two (2) scores are added to the score of the superior judge and divided by three (3).

	Average	Spread
18.3.1.1	9.0 and above	2/10
18.3.1.2	8.5-8.95	3/10
18.3.1.3	8.45 and below	5/10

18.3.2 If a judge consistently shows himself to be incompetent in his duty he must be removed by the superior judge.

C. JURY

19. The Jury consists of:

19.1	Superior judge	1
19.2	Judges for execution 4 (Nos. 1-4)	4
19.3	Judges for difficulty 2 (Nos. 5-6)	2
19.4	Total	7

20. Duties of the Superior Judge

20.1 Control of the facilities.

20.2 Organization of the judge's conference and the trial scoring.

20.3 Drawing for the starting order.

20.4 Directing the competition.

20.5 Placing and supervising all judges.

20.6 Supervising all the spotters.

20.7 Informing the performance judges Nos. 1-4 of the deductions as per rule 9.4.

20.8 Determining if a competitor leaves the mat and notifying the judges Nos. 1-4 and difficulty judges Nos. 5-6.

20.9 Ruling on the competitor's clothing.

20.10 Personally scoring the performance of each pass. His score sheet is handed to the recorder before he verifies the scores of judges Nos. 1-4.

20.11 Deciding if a judge fails to show his score immediately as per No. 18.2.5.

20.12 Supervising judges Nos. 5-6 and deciding if there is a difference in the degree of difficulty of a pass.

20.13 Control of the total score.

20.14 To inform judges Nos. 1-4 of 2.0 for each skill omitted from the compulsory pass.

20.15 To inform judges Nos. 1-4 of the following cumulative deductions for the voluntary passes:

    20.15.1 Not doing the required type of pass as per rules 4.1.2, 4.1.3, and 4.2.1   2.0

    20.15.2 Less than two (2) somersaults in a pass.   .5

    20.15.3 Pass without a somersault.   2.0

    20.15.4 Failure to end a pass with a somersault.   .5

20.16 Deciding when a competitor's pass has begun.

20.17 Deciding about the removal of an incompetent judge.

20.18 Informing the recorder and judges Nos. 1-4 of a zero (0) score for less than three (3) skills in a pass.

21. Duties of the Judges for Performance (1-4)

    21.1 The judges must sit separately 5 m from the side of the tumbling mat.

    21.2 Scores for performance shall range from 0.0 to 10.0 pt. per pass.

    21.3 Deductions for faulty performance

        21.3.1 Slight faults

        Small and insignificant deviations from the perfect performance as described by the following:

        A slight delay in rhythm, a small deviation from the center of mat (30 cm either direction), untight tuck or pike, legs apart when not required, unpointed feet and toes, or knee bends of less than 10 degrees in layout or pike somersault, heavy landings on feet or hands, final landing with a bounce or steps. Deduct for each occurrence of a slight fault 1/10 to 3/10.

        21.3.2 Substantial faults

        Noticeable and essential deviations from perfect performance as described by the following:

        A substantial delay or change in rhythm; deviation from the center of the mat to either edge; the final somersault in a pass rotating below shoulder height; touching the floor with the hands after somersault landings; insufficient momentum after round-offs, hand springs, and somersaults in order to properly execute the following skill; bad landings; knee bends of 10 degrees or more, in layout or pike somersault; underspin or overspin of twists and somersault of 45 degrees or less. Deduct for each occurrence of a substantial fault 4/10 to 6/10.

21.3.3 Major faults
Large deviations or distortions in technique and execution of skills or skill combinations as described by the following:
The loss of speed to near standstill; going off the side of the mat with either hand or foot; deep squat on handsprings, round-offs and flick-flacks; somersaults nearly touching the floor; underspin or overspin of twists by more than 45 degrees and falling. Deduct for each occurrence of major fault 7/10 to 1.0.

21.3.4 Leniency for unusual difficulty or virtuosity
Mitigation from 0.1-0.3 can be made in the deductions of faults on skills or skill combinations which in the opinion of the judge are unusually difficult or a pass which shows exceptional virtuosity.

22. Duties of the Difficulty Judges (Nos. 5-6)
22.1 Determining the difficulty of each pass and skill and entering it on the competition card.
22.2 Displaying the difficulty mark.
22.3 Deducting the difficulty value of excessive skills as per rule 16.1.

glossary

A. A. U.: The Amateur Athletic Union is the international sanctioning unit for all U. S. teams in matches between nations.

Active Spotting: A safety technique whereby the coach or spotter assists the tumbler through the trick, from takeoff until landing.

Aerials: Any tumbling movement where the performer rotates 360 degrees from feet to feet.

Aerial Cartwheel: A cartwheel performed without touching the hands on the mat.

Aerial Walkover: A front walkover without touching the hands on the mat.

All-Around: A term used to describe competition in all of the Olympic events in gymnastics.

Alternations: A series of tumbling tricks, either forward or backward, where somersaults are "alternated" with handsprings or headsprings.

"A" Moves: In F. I. G. rules the easiest classification or least difficult type of movement or trick.

Apparatus: A term used to describe the equipment used in gymnastics competition, including bars and rings.

Arabian: A half twist to a front somersault.

Axis: An imaginary line around which the body will turn or rotate during tumbling or gymnastics movements.

"Back": A somersault or flip performed backwards, somersaulting 360 degrees from feet to feet.

Back Extension: A variation of kip movements where the tumbler rolls backwards and ends the movement in a handstand.

Back Handspring: The most important fundamental tumbling trick where the athlete flips backwards from feet, to hands, then to feet again.

Backward Roll: A basic tumbling movement where the tumbler rolls backward 360 degrees without leaving contact with the floor.

Baranie: A half-twisting front flip usually performed with the body in an "open" or "semi-piked" position.

Blocking: A technique where the tumbler converts forward or backward momentum to height by exerting a downward thrust with the legs or arms.

"B" Moves: In international gymnastics the middle or moderately difficult class of movement.

Bottoming-out: A term used to describe what happens when a tumbler's feet strike the floor through a tumbling mat that is too soft.

Bounders: Two or more consecutive flips performed without any intermediary handsprings or headsprings.

Cartwheel: A beginning tumbling move where the athlete rotates sidewards from feet to hands to feet.

Center of Gravity: The "theoretical" point where the body weight is centered or evenly distributed above and below.

"C" Moves: In F. I. G. rules the hardest or most difficult classification of movement.

Combination(s): In the singular form, a work representing certain requirements that must be met to score well under F. I. T. or F. I. G. rules; in the plural form, a word representing the actual variety of tricks used in specific routines.

Conditioning: The activities and exercises used to increase strength and endurance for more effective tumbling.

Crash-pad: A soft mat made of foam rubber used to cushion falls while learning dangerous or new tricks.

Cross-tumbling: An old requirement in tumbling rules where the athlete was required to end one tumbling run in a handstand position.

Cushion: A mistake in technique where the tumbler loses or dissipates power by allowing the body to bend and absorb energy.

Dive Roll: A forward roll where the initial action is to jump or dive up and out, covering a large distance in the air before the hands touch the mat.

Double Back: A backward somersaulting trick where the tumbler rotates twice around the horizontal axis extending from hip to hip.

Double Front: A forward somersaulting trick where the tumbler rotates twice around the horizontal axis extending from hip to hip.

Double Full: A backward, twisting somersault where the tumbler rotates once around the horizontal axis and twice around the vertical axis, which extends from head to toe.

Double Twisting Front: A forward, twisting flip where the tumbler rotates once around the horizontal axis and twice around the vertical axis.

F. I. G.: International Gymnastics Federation, the worldwide governing body for the sport of gymnastics.

F. I. T.: International Tumbling Federation, the worldwide governing body for the sport of tumbling.

Flexibility: A term used to describe a better than average range of motion in the major joints of the body.

Flic-Flac: See Back handspring.

Fliffis: Any double somersault with at least 180 degrees of twisting around the vertical axis.

Flip: See Somersault.

Flip-Flop: See Back handspring.

Floor Exercises: An event in men's and women's gymnastics performed on a 40-foot by 40-foot mat and incorporating leaps, holds, strength, flexibility, and tumbling movements.

Forward Roll: A basic tumbling movement where the athlete rolls forward 360 degrees without breaking contact with the floor.

Front: A term used to describe forward flips where the tumbler rotates forward 360 degrees in the air from feet to feet.

Full Twist: A backward somersault where the tumbler also rotates 360 degrees around the vertical axis from head to toe.

Gymnastics: In ancient Greece a term used to describe all physical sport skills, today a specific sport involving rings, bars, horse, vaulting, etc.

Half: A term usually referring to a one-half rotation around the vertical axis.

Half-in, Half-out: A type of fliffis where one half twist is performed on each somersault.

Handstand: A balance movement where the tumbler balances with the body straight above the hands.

Handspot: A spotting or safety technique where the coach manipulates the tumbler with his hands only.

Handspring: A basic tumbling movement where the athlete flips from feet, to hands, to feet (usually forward).

Headspring: A basic tumbling movement that is also a variation of kip movements performed from feet to head and hands to feet.

Horizontal Axis: The imaginary line extending from one hip to another around which the body flips or somersaults.

Hurdle Step: A "set-up jump" resembling a skip that allows the tumbler to place the power leg in front for round-offs, handsprings, etc.

Kip: A basic gymnastics movement where the athlete changes body position by first "piking," then forcefully extending the body.

Kip-up: A variation of kips where the tumbler rolls back in a pike, then extends the body and arms and lands on his feet.

Landing Mat: A safety mat made of medium-dense foam and used to cushion the landing shock on the legs after extremely high stunts.

Layout: A flipping position where the tumbler's body is extending from head to feet throughout the somersault.

Leotard: An elastic one-piece garment for women used predominantly in dance, gymnastics, and tumbling.

Lift-back: A backward somersault where the tumbler tries to raise the center of gravity as high as possible.

Mat: The surface composed of resilient material on which tumblers and gymnasts perform.

Mounter: A unique type of tumbling movement that requires a high lift in the first half and extreme flexibility in the second half.

Mule-kick: A position movement that increases the tumbler's ability to perform backward handsprings. Beginning in a handstand position snap the feet downward onto the floor and rebound back to the handstand position.

Novice: A newcomer, young student, beginner, or inexperienced participant in the sport.

Overhead Spotting Rig: A piece of safety equipment that consists of a belt with ropes run through pulleys attached to the ceiling.

Pass: One segment of a tumbling routine consisting of one trip down the mat with at least three consecutive tricks.

Passive Spotting: A safety technique where the coach or spotter allows the tumbler to complete the movement alone, intervening only if he senses the tumbler is in trouble.

Pike: A somersaulting position where the tumbler bends only at the hips and keeps the knees straight.

Pirouette: A full 360-degree rotation around the vertical axis without any somersault.

Positive Movement: The tumbling concept that requires the athlete to maintain straight line momentum down the length of the tumbling mat.

Power Leg: The forward leg after the hurdle step, always the strongest leg for each tumbler.

Power Tumbling: The technique incorporating fast flip-flops, achieved by bending and straightening the arms at the elbow joint.

Progressions: A teaching method that involves breaking each trick down into component parts, mastering each part before attempting the entire trick.

Psyched-out: A term tumblers and gymnasts use to describe a general feeling of insecurity or fear about learning a new trick or routine; a lack of confidence.

Reuther System: A newly developed tumbling surface, composed of wood supported by wood leaf springs, that gives the athletes more height.

Rotation: Usually used to describe the movement initiated around the horizontal axis in flips or somersaults.

Round-off: A basic tumbling skill that changes forward momentum to backward momentum by the performance of a one-half twist from feet to hands to feet.

Routine: A tumbling routine may consist of as few as three runs or as many as five or six runs.

R.O.V.: An abbreviation for risk, originality, and virtuosity, aspects that quality tumbling and gymnastics routines must demonstrate to score high.

Rudolf: A slang term for a one-and-one-half twisting front somersault, a trick of superior difficulty on floor.

Run: See Pass.

Salto: The F.I.G. and F.I.T. official term for somersault or flip.

Set: See Routine.

"Side Somy": A somersault performed in a sideward direction from feet to feet covering 360 degrees.

Scale: A balance and flexibility trick, one of the position movements; also any hold positions where only one foot is in contact with the ground.

Sokol: Originally a Slavic-based athletic/social organization that was instrumental in the beginning and growth of gymnastics and tumbling in the United States.

Somersault: Any stunt where the athlete rotates around a horizontal axis 360 degrees from feet to feet completely in the air; "somy," "flip," etc.

Splits: A flexibility movement where the tumbler shows superior range of motion in the legs and hips.

Spotter: Anyone who aids a tumbler in the performance of a new or risky stunt so as to prevent injury.

Spotting: The assistance of a performer during a movement in order to speed learning and prevent injury.

Spotting Belt: A canvas belt with ropes that can be held by spotters to prevent injuries.

Step-out: The action of landing on one foot after a somersault so as to continue immediately into a trick requiring a one foot takeoff.

Stretching: Any action that safely increases the flexibility or range of motion in the joints of the body.

Stretch Position: Usually refers to the extended, tight position of the body during certain moves (*e.g.,* handstands, layouts).

Tigna: A forward somersault with a one-foot takeoff to a step-out landing, sometimes incorporating a ¼ twist between takeoff and landing.

Tinsica: Very similar to front handsprings except the hands are staggered and the landing is one foot at a time.

Trajectory: The line of flight between the takeoff and landing during any somersault.

Triple Full: A backward twisting somersault where the tumbler rotates once around the horizontal axis and three times around the vertical axis.

Tuck: A somersaulting position where the athlete's knees are curled into the chest and the back is rounded, the arms holding the legs.

Turnverein: A German social/athletic organization that, along with the Sokol, was instrumental in the formation of gymnastics in the United States.

Twisting: Rotation around the vertical axis extending from the head to feet.

Twisting Mechanic: A spotting belt set up to allow the tumbler to twist and flip simultaneously.

U.S.T.A.: The United States Trampoline Association, a recently formed body that governs the sport of rebound tumbling or trampolining non-international matches.

Vertical Axis: The imaginary line around which the body twists that extends from head to feet.

Walkovers: Fundamental movements that require flexibility in the lower back as tumblers slowly turn from feet, to hands, to feet.

Whip Back: A fast backward somersault performed in an open position with the center of gravity kept low.

Y. M. C. A.: Young Men's Christian Association, in cooperation with A. A. U., helped to foster early tumbling competition.

index